MW00898297

The Teachings of Jesus

—

New Thoughts on the Gospels'
Principles, Prayers and Parables
by Glenn Chaffin

—

ISBN-13:978-1500560171
ISBN-10:1500560170

TABLE OF CONTENTS

DEDICATION

I wrote this book for free-thinkers of every denomination, for even in the most orthodox and conservative religions there are open-minded seekers of Truth and wisdom who have the courage to confront the challenge of a new thought. This book is dedicated to those students, and to those who remember hearing the teachings of Jesus, but have turned away from what was being taught. It is intended for those who think that the teachings of Jesus cannot be reconciled with their spirituality, their liberality, and their rejection of religion. This book is dedicated to those who have thrown the baby out with the bathwater! Students of New Thought need not ignore the teachings of Jesus, even though they reject the doctrines commonly associated with them.

Eckhart von Hochheim, better known as Meister Eckhart, a fourteenth century Dominican priest, theologian, and philosopher was posthumously excommunicated because of the heretical tone of his teachings. One quote ascribed to him is: "If the only prayer you ever said in your entire life was thank you, it would suffice." At this late date I would like to thank my family, friends and students whose patience with me and my endeavors is to be rewarded with this small volume of thoughts and ideas — all of which they have heard before.

Rev. Glenn Chaffin
Summer, 2014
Minnesota

PREFACE

Thank You

Before anything is said or read, before facing the task at hand, the first thing to do is give thanks: Thank you. This simple acknowledgment makes us mindful of all that we have, and puts us in a frame of mind to accept more. Thus, a prayer of thanks can serve as a good preface to whatever we are about to turn our attention to.

However, why say anything at all? Why try to express gratitude in words? Why make a show of our sincere appreciation by praying aloud? Why not keep those thoughts to oneself, where they may do more good? Is "Thank you" spoken aloud because it needs to be said, or because someone needs to hear it? I can recall only two instances in the Gospels where Jesus uttered a public prayer. On one of those occasions, Jesus states that he spoke aloud to get a response from the public, not from God. The verse tells us that Jesus lifted up his eyes, and said: "Father, I thank thee that thou hast heard me. And I knew that thou hearest me always: but because of the people which stand by I said *it,* that they may believe that thou hast sent me." (Jn. 11:41-42 KJV)

I must admit it is quite reasonable that public prayers are spoken to sway public opinion, and I would not find these motivational monologues so objectionable if they were not considered prayers. To do so degrades prayer to an act of subtle argument and manipulation. Once we accept the sanctity of praying over people at public gatherings we begin to believe our prayer wields those same powers of persuasion over God. It does not, and anyone who understands a prayer in this way has misunderstood their relationship with the Divine. If our relationship to God is personal, I think our prayer ought to be private, not public. I do not think that prayer is a valid way to change anyone's mind, except my own.

Perhaps the perfect prayer is, Thank God; for when it comes to public prayers, the less said, the better. The more said, the less perfect our prayers become. By giving thanks, Jesus affirmed his belief that God answers our prayers before we pray. He obviously knew the verse in the Old Testament Book of Isaiah which attributes this statement to God: "And it shall come to pass, that before they call, I will answer; and while they are yet speaking, I will hear." (Is. 65:24) Before we ask, the gift is given. Before we pray, our prayer is answered.

Jesus also taught that public prayers were hypocritical and counter-productive in that they do not get a response from God: "And when thou prayest, thou shalt not be as the hypocrites *are*: for they love to pray standing in the synagogues and in the corners of the streets, that they may be seen of men. Verily I say unto you, They have their reward." (Mt. 6:5) So, why would he pray, in a way, that others could see and hear? It was not to reinforce his own faith, but to encourage their belief in him. It was all for show. All public prayer is part of the show. So though it is good to show appreciation to others, it is the attitude of gratitude that gives meaning to our words. If the consciousness of gratitude is not already established within, then prayer is spoken in vain. Once one is at the point of accepting, then there is nothing more to ask for. Just shut the door and thank God.

"But thou, when thou prayest, enter into thy closet, and when thou hast shut thy door, pray to thy Father which is in secret; and thy Father which seeth in secret shall reward thee openly." (Mt. 6:6)

Why

Before reading any further, ask: Why? Why reconsider the teachings of Jesus? What more could be said about them, or found within them? Why try to find new insights and understanding in verses that others have studied for thousands of years? It is precisely because thousands of years of study have not exhausted this discourse that we can expect to find new thoughts and our own insights.

There is a distinction to be made, between thinking you know something and knowing what you think. However don't bother reviewing these teachings in hopes of finding a winning argument, or a way to answer Biblical scholars (family, friends and neighbors at the door) who seek to convert you to their way of thinking. There is very little chance of that. This commentary on the teachings of Jesus provides no arguments, no ammo or bullet points to defend against such offensive behavior; although, reading this book may put a stop to it. I found that when I didn't know what I believed, there were plenty of people ready to tell me why I should think like them. The proponents of salvation found me to be an easy opponent. However, once I knew what I thought, no one bothered to ask me what I think. They were not interested in what I thought, but only in telling me what to think. I would rather put an end to such conversion conversations than try to win those debates. I would rather read and think about the teachings of Jesus than argue about it with anyone else; so I just say thank you, as I shut the door.

No one can think for you, but until you think for yourself, they'll keep trying. The apostle Paul wrote: "And be not conformed to this world: but be ye transformed by the renewing of your mind, that ye may prove what is that good, and acceptable, and perfect, will of God." (Rm. 12:2) Pay attention to the personal pronouns in that verse. It is up to you to not be a conformist. It is up to you to transform your mind. It is your life that must prove what you think; which makes all testimony, debate and argument unnecessary.

Reading is an activity well suited to renewing one's mind, for it provides an opportunity for the reader to change their own mind, or not as they choose. If you are open to considering some new thoughts, which may inspire your own insights and understanding, then read on.

INTRODUCTION

A New Thought

In the United States, beginning in the last half of the nineteenth century, a philosophical, spiritual healing, self-help, religious movement organized around the idea that by changing your mind, you can change your life. They called it New Thought, though its teachers and preachers reached back to Jesus for their spiritual principles. The only thing new about it was its embrace of new scientific theories and disciplines in promoting a holistic approach to the health, wealth and well-being of the individual. New Thought is no longer new. If it ever had a new thought, its message is not new any longer. It has been mainstreamed in the guise of positive thinking and self-esteem. However, once anything is old enough to be forgotten, once it is out of sight and out of mind, it becomes new again. It is as true of thought as it is of things because it is true of us: the only new thought is the one that is new to you.

There are no new thoughts waiting around to be found. There is only an eventual recognition of eternal truths. A thought is new to you when first realized, but don't think you are the first to grasp it. I recently became aware of the Dominican theologian, Giordano Bruno, who was put to death by the Inquisition in 1600 a.d. for professing his belief in an infinite God, in an infinite universe, in which all is One. He offended the religious authorities by telling them that though they professed a belief in a supreme Being, their concept of God just wasn't big enough! No matter how great you think God is -- if we think of God and man instead of God as man then we are not thinking big enough. If we think of Heaven and Earth instead of Heaven on Earth, our Heaven is too small. If we worship the Father and the Son instead of realizing, "I and *my* Father are one" (Jn. 10:30), then our beliefs limit our spirituality. If we think when is then, instead of now, we have a limited grasp of reality.

I wish I had learned of Bruno's writings earlier in my life because for decades I've professed the same concepts he died for, under the delusion that these insights originated with me. They originated within me, but they were not original with me. There are no truly new thoughts, only thoughts that are new to you.

Common Sense

I'd like to say that the following pages offer a common-sense commentary on the teachings of Jesus, but they do not. My comments are not only uncommon in their content, but also in their lack of denominational precepts. The common approach to Gospel commentary is an attempt to make sense of Jesus' teachings from one's own religious perspective; which may explain why common sense is an uncommon thing in the field of religion and spirituality.

When reading the Bible, we tend to reason from our beliefs, rather than to a reasonable belief. We tend to limit our consideration of what to believe to what we already believe, as presented by those with whom we usually agree. One usually studies the teachings of Jesus in the context of some other book of religious teachings, presented as another chapter, an appendix to what one is supposed to think. That reinforces preconceived notions of what is right and true, confirming that one is right to believe as they do. If we are not careful to distinguish between what we believe to be true, and how these truths are used to justify what we do, we tend toward self-righteousness rather than the righteousness of doing the right thing. Most Gospel commentaries use the teachings of Jesus as an argument in favor of a particular religious doctrine. However, my favorite religion has no doctrines that rely on Jesus' endorsement. So, I will not make an appeal to scriptures for support of what to do, but for inspiration and as an explanation of why I think as I do.

7

Principles and Doctrines

Most Christian denominations would not have me as a member, and rightfully so, since I do not ascribe to their precepts and practices. Even so, I consider myself a Christian, although of the New Thought persuasion. I do not think one can be a student of New Thought if they reject the principles Jesus taught. New Thought principles are not founded on Gospel verses, but they can be found there. Mind you, I am talking about principles, not denominational doctrines. Most of what is taught about the teachings of Jesus is not what Jesus taught. Jesus taught principles. Doctrines are what others thought about what Jesus taught. Principles are meant to be understood. Doctrines are meant to be followed. Doctrines tell people what to do when they do not know what to do, but when you understand the principle involved, you know what you must do, and how to do it. For example, Jesus' teachings would make for a very difficult doctrine of love: "But I say unto you, Love your enemies, bless them that curse you, do good to them that hate you, and pray for them which despitefully use you, and persecute you." (Mt. 5:44)

If we understand the fundamental premise of this verse, we will be able to practice the principle of being loving, and be able to bless, give and forgive anyone. That is what Jesus would do, but that has never been in question. The real question is: What am I to be? The answer to that question may be found in Mt. 5:20-48. Those twenty-nine verses are a lot to consider, but it gets us to this point: "Be ye therefore perfect, even as your Father which is in heaven is perfect." (Mt. 5:48)

Perhaps you've heard the doctrine that we are to love and forgive one another because, after all, we are only human, and it would be hypocritical of us not to. Perhaps you've accepted the doctrine that nobody is perfect, except God, and maybe Jesus. However, he taught that you are to be perfect in the same way God

8

is. You can be perfect because you are perfect; you just don't know how. When you do not know how *(the principle)*, knowing what to do *(the doctrine)* is of little use. To know how to love and bless and forgive requires the recognition of perfection. We do not love and forgive others because they are only human, but because we are all perfect spiritual beings. Jesus ridiculed those who thought of themselves as only human, just flesh and bone. (See Jn. 8:56-58) He considered himself to be an eternal spiritual being, and would have us all understand the eternality of our spirituality: "Verily, verily, I say unto you, Before Abraham was, I am." (Jn. 8:58)

Italicized Text

Scriptural quotations used herein are from the authorized King James version of the Bible. It can be difficult to read transcriptions, which were translated into the now antiquated English of that period, without the benefit of quotation marks and other punctuations to aid understanding. Even so, I prefer the King James Version because it requires that one study obscure words to understand the meaning of the verse. Otherwise, one must accept the best efforts of well-meaning translators, who by modernizing the grammar and vocabulary, make changes that sometimes change the meaning of the verse.

For example, as you read the scriptures, take note of the words that appear in italics. Scribes and translators have added the italicized words to restore what was missing from the text, and in an attempt to explain what they thought others might misunderstand. Jn. 10:30 is a sample of such an attempt at either grammatical or theological correctness, which I find objectionable. Jesus did not speak of God as his Father; or rather, not his alone. The scribe could have taken a cue from the Lord's Prayer, inserting *our* instead of *my*. Jesus did not teach us to pray to his Father. He taught that we should begin prayer with the concept: "Our Father, …" Such an all-inclusive salutation expresses a consciousness of oneness with God, and with one another. That is all a prayer must do to have a positive affect. However, enough on that, for I am digressing into commentary before finishing my introduction!

Inspiration

Though my thoughts may be uncommon, they follow a common theme and fundamental truth of Jesus' teachings: oneness with God. I find that by realizing our oneness with God that we are able to make sense of what Jesus taught. Even so, I must admit that my approach is all too common. I too have a religious point of view from which I read the teachings of Jesus. However, it is not my intent to present well-worn truths in support of my religious beliefs. I am not interested in used truths, or how these truths have been used to justify beliefs, doctrines and dogma. I intend to provide a new thought on eternal truths as expressed in the teachings of Jesus.

These truths are not new, and some of my thoughts about them echo statements by other, much older, thinkers of new thoughts. Nevertheless, these ideas were new to me, and they may be news to you. As everyone's perspective is unique to themselves, one persons' views may appear rather peculiar to others. Thus, a new thought is always uncommon and must seem odd at first, even when it is your own. In this sense, there can be no common sense where insights are considered. There can be common books of prayers, doctrines we hold in common with others, agreements, covenants and shared beliefs, but inspiration will always be an uncommon awareness. The Truth is never a new idea, but the inspiration it reveals is always a new thought.

THE BE ATTITUDES
Matthew 5:1-12

And seeing the multitudes, he went up into a mountain: and when he was set, his disciples came unto him: And he opened his mouth, and taught them, saying,

Blessed *are* the poor in spirit:

for theirs is the kingdom of heaven.

Blessed *are* they that mourn:

for they shall be comforted.

Blessed *are* the meek:

for they shall inherit the earth.

Blessed *are* they which do hunger and thirst after righteousness:

for they shall be filled.

Blessed *are* the merciful:

for they shall obtain mercy.

Blessed *are* the pure in heart:

for they shall see God.

Blessed *are* the peacemakers:

for they shall be called the children of God.

Blessed *are* they which are persecuted for righteousness sake: for theirs is the kingdom of heaven. Blessed are ye, when men shall revile you, and persecute you, and shall say all manner of evil against you falsely, for my sake. Rejoice, and be exceeding glad: for great is your reward in heaven: for so persecuted they the prophets which were before you.

Uncommon Sense

Throughout the teachings of Jesus we find many statements, which conflict with common sense, statements such as: "... love your enemies, bless them that curse you, do good to them that hate you, and pray for them which despitefully use you, and persecute you;" (Mt. 5:44) Verses like these are found throughout the Gospels because Jesus did not teach common sense, but spiritual principles that require us to see beyond appearances.

It takes an uncommon attitude to practice the principles he taught. We might well ask, who could be expected to agree with their adversary? (See Mt. 5:25) Who could forgive, not just seven times, but seventy times seven? (See Mt. 18:25)

The Gospels confirm that Jesus practiced what he preached. However, the challenge is not in believing Jesus could do it, but that we can. Jesus began the Sermon on the Mount by listing eight qualities of thought and the blessed state of mind that accompanies them. The correlation is clear for most of the eight: What we ask for, we receive, and the way we think becomes our experience.

It may not be obvious, but our blessing is not a future reward. Our blessing is concurrent with the attitude we express. Therefore, it is better that we give thanks for what we've got than to bemoan what we have not. It is better that we affirm that we are blessed than to digress. After all, if we don't think that we are blessed, can it ever be so? If we don't think that we are blessed, perhaps we are not. If it is done unto us as we believe, then we had better believe that what is being done unto us carries a blessing!

The Beatitudes describe in a variety of ways the one benefit of living a spiritually principled life: we get to experience the Spirit of Life. That doesn't happen if we live according to the wisdom of the world as taught in the School of Hard Knocks. Instead of relying on experience alone, the wise rely on insight gained from their experience of Life. They affirm that they are blessed regardless of the experience.

THE POOR SPIRITED

Blessed *are* the poor in spirit: for theirs is the kingdom of
heaven.

Mt. 5:3

Poor in Spirit

I don't know what it means to be poor, let alone poor in spirit;
nevertheless, I don't like the sound of it! Most people strive to
thrive and prosper in all ways, and do not wish to be poor in any
way. And that is reasonable, for we must live our life as a whole,
and poverty in one aspect of our life would diminish the richness
of the whole of our life. So, the only reason to wish to be poor is if,
on the whole, this poverty would enrich one's life. But can a way
of life that enriches the whole of your life be properly considered
poverty?

Some Biblical scholars interpret "poor" to mean financial
poverty, incurred for the sake of finding spiritual "wealth." They
suggest that by choosing physical and financial impoverishment,
one is compensated with non-material wealth. In this ascetic
approach to life, it is their choice and their dedication that holds
the promise of spiritual richness. They are not suffering for the
sake of suffering, or doing without just to see how much they can
do without. They choose to live poorly in order to enrich their
lives. Those who are born into poverty, or fall into poverty, would
not then be considered poor in spirit; they would in fact be poor,
but not in the spirit.

Others teach that being poor in spirit refers to a vow of poverty
for the sake of pursuing a higher calling: being poor for Heaven's
sake. In this instance, poverty would be more accurately termed a
not for profit approach to life. The profits of one's labor and
constant fund-raising are plowed back into the spiritual pursuit
rather than profiting one personally. Such an approach to being

poor in spirit can be financially rewarding, providing a comfortable living for those who devote themselves to it.

Still other scholars say that the poor in spirit are those who wish to rely wholly on God. It is not clear if these poor souls are relying on divine intervention to supply manna from the heavens and water flowing from rocks, or if they rely solely on God to supply their wants and needs, through the charity of those who don't rely solely on God.

These interpretations seem reasonable, and they also find support from other verses found in the teachings of Jesus. However, any assertion that one has reason to believe will sound reasonable, and a Bible verse can be found in support of any idea you can imagine. Some even think it reasonable to interpret Matthew 5:3 to state that hose who have little money now will be compensated with heavenly riches later. (Those who want a little of your money teach that version.)

Spiritual Compensation

Jesus does assert that the poor in spirit have a spiritual wealth: "… theirs is the kingdom of heaven." This juxtaposition of poverty and wealth lends support to the idea that being poor in spirit is a decision motivated by a desire to realize spiritual wealth. This way of thinking is well represented in the lyrics of the song, I Got Plenty O' Nuttin by George Gershwin:

> I got plenty of nothing
> And nothing's plenty for me
> I got no car — got no mule
> I got no misery
> Folks with plenty of plenty
> They've got a lock on the door
> Afraid somebody's gonna rob 'em
> While there out making more

14

— what for
I got no lock on the door
— that's no way to be
They can steal the rug from the floor
— that's ok with me
'cause the things that I prize
— like the stars in the skies
— are all free
I got plenty of nothing
And nothing's plenty for me
I got my gal — got my song
got heaven the whole day long
— got my gal
— got my love
— got my song

If only it were that easy; however, financial poverty does not
necessarily lead to spiritual wealth. There are plenty of poor people
who are not rich in spirit. And, there are plenty of indigent people
who are spiritually wealthy. Are they rich in spirit because they are
financially poor, or in spite of it? Is their spiritual richness a
compensation, a consolation, for their financial poverty? Or are
they rich in spirit because the kingdom of God is within them, and
they know it? Is it theirs, because they are poor? Or, is it
there, whether they are poor or not?

Jesus began his Sermon on the Mount by challenging the
common notion of what it means to be blessed. Then it was
believed that those who prosper — who have benefits, have more
than enough, are generously compensated, richly rewarded, cup
running over with abundance — have been blessed by God, the
source of all goods. The corollary to that belief was that those who
were not so blessed were, in fact, judged by God and condemned
to suffer a life of poverty. Prosperity was a sign of being in God's

favor and crop failure, or a similar loss, was a clear indication of being out of favor. Success was the reward of righteousness, and suffering was punishment for sin. Jesus contradicted this correlation of wealth and righteousness by suggesting that it is actually the poor who are in God's favor: "… for theirs is the kingdom of heaven."

If one is seeking followers to challenge the status quo, then a popular idea is essential; but what was he suggesting? Is it that the poor are blessed by God? Was he suggesting that wealth is not a reward of righteousness? Was he suggesting that the wealthy are not necessarily righteous, while the poor are righteous, by virtue of their poverty? Those who appear to lead a blessed life are often viewed with suspicion and held in contempt, by those who think themselves to be poorer in comparison. Those who consider themselves to be poor, sometimes think they are more righteous than those who prosper and succeed in life.

In challenging the traditional view that wealth is a reward of righteousness, I don't think Jesus was suggesting that poverty is the reward. Jesus was not promoting a social revolution. He was rejecting the religious correlation of wealth with righteousness. Jesus spoke of being blessed as a condition of one's soul, not the physical conditions in which one lives. Even so, if the conditions in which one lives are so bad as to turn his attention away from the world, then perhaps that person should consider himself blessed; for the person who turns within and perceives the presence of God in his life is blessed!

THE MOURNFUL

Blessed *are* they that mourn: for they shall be comforted.
Mt. 5:4

Consciousness is the Compensation

The blessed are not those who appear to have it all, or think they have it all. Nor, are the blessed those who forsake it all for the sake of forsaking it all. Among the blessed are those who are poor in spirit, mournful, meek, hungry and persecuted for their righteousness. One might be tempted to thank Jesus for the warning and try to avoid such a blessing; however, that would make matters worse.

No one wishes to be in mourning; even so, those who mourn are blessed — they are comforted. Mourning is asking for and accepting comfort. If one won't mourn, but instead ignores their loss, then they cannot be comforted. Comforting compensates for their mourning. It does not redress their loss, but it can alleviate their suffering.

Suffering

Jesus did not teach that we should suffer but that we could do something to ease our suffering. We should mourn our loss. Suffering is not mourning. Morning puts an end to suffering. To suffer is to continue with or in a situation, not to put an end to it. Lately, it is only used in the context of hardship, but it is not limited to that. Jesus gave an injunction to the disciples: "Suffer little children, and forbid them not, to come unto me; for of such is the kingdom of heaven." (Mt. 19:14) He didn't mean that children bring suffering, but that we are to let the children continue being children even though they are disruptive.

A time of mourning is meant to put an end to suffering (continued hardship). In hard times, it is unwise to think that you will lessen your suffering by not allowing yourself to mourn. In fact, you will prolong and increase your suffering. Times will change, but that doesn't change your mind or your emotions. Those who will not mourn a loss will carry that loss forward until they finally give an accounting of it, and by then it has increased with interest.

Mourning

It is wise and necessary to mourn, for it marks the willingness to be comforted. When we refuse to mourn we are trying to avoid the loss, not to think about it, not feel it. We suspect that mourning would just make matters worse; however, refusing to mourn would be like closing the barn door after the horse has run away.

Be advised: prolonged mourning does not prolong the comfort. Being comforted has a point of diminishing returns. Prolonged comforting becomes pampering, which if continued will begin to chaff our soul. We must begin our healing and rehabilitation as soon as possible. The blessing of mourning is not its duration but rather its culmination. Mourning is the acceptance, or knowledge, that one experience must be left in the past for a new and wonderful day is dawning. What an opportunity it is to be at rock-bottom and know that now you have reached a foundation upon which you can build.

Accept and Release

If you think your life just isn't working out as it might have, it is understandable that you will mourn the lost possibility; for deep within you is the belief that it need not have been so. Nevertheless, do not be bitter about the past or angry, at this moment, with yourself or anyone else. Accept and release: this is the essence of mourning. It is as necessary and natural as inhaling and exhaling. Accept the loss, and release yourself from it. Accept yourself and release the death grip of fear and control.

Comfort

Those who mourn are comforted because mourning marks the end of suffering our loss. Comfort comes as suffering concludes. Comfort comes as you perceive that life goes on, and as you continue along with it. It is comforting to perceive an answer or find a better question. Answers bring a sense of comfort as they resolve questions. The answer that is always comforting is the awareness of the presence of Life within you, as you. There is no loss in an infinite universe. What we consider to be a loss is transition, or transformation; not a loss at all. We lose sight of that which we cherish, but this only serves to point out another horizon. To find comfort in this, we must be transformed by the renewing of our mind.

THE MEEK

> Blessed *are* the meek, for they shall inherit the earth.
> Mt. 5:5

Blessed Attitudes

Blessed, as used in the Beatitudes connotes supreme happiness, the realization of good fortune. That is a stark contrast to the physical conditions described. We do not usually consider mourning to be a time of good fortune or happiness; nor is it at all clear that the meek, and the persecuted will prevail. Even so, to make his point very clearly, Jesus presents this juxtaposition of a worldly point of view with spiritual principles. The meek are gentle, courteous, and kind. In a violent, aggressive and competitive world, these qualities may appear to be naive; therefore, the meek cannot afford to be stupid. Jesus further clarified this point: "Behold, I send you forth as sheep in the midst of wolves: be ye therefore wise as serpents, and harmless as doves." (Mt.10:16)

Meekness has a connotation of submissiveness and victimization, though it is more accurately a passive and peaceful approach to living. The blessed are meek, for they contend with none and when the fighting is done they find that they have won. It appears that the aggressors rule the world, but those who live by the sword die by the sword and only the meek are left to inherit the earth.

Inheritance

It does not appear that the meek inherit the world. It seems that the most aggressive individuals always end up on the top, taking the lion's share so to speak. Are we to believe that when the aggressors kill themselves off, the meek will finally get their inheritance? It hasn't worked out that way because the lions prey upon the lambs, not one another. But this misses the point.

- The meek do not inherit the lion's share.
- The meek do not trade places with the aggressors.
- The meek do not inherit the spoils of war.

I think we can assume that Jesus was familiar with the Book of Psalms and knew that the earth doesn't belong to the aggressors. "The earth is the LORD'S, and the fulness thereof; the world, and they that dwell therein". (Psalm 24:1) Does one inherit from a vanquished foe, or our Father? The gift of Life doesn't belong to those who take it, but to those who accept it: the meek.

Shepherd and Lamb

Jesus equated himself with a lamb rather than a lion; and here we find the model for meekness. The lamb is meek in its willingness to be cared for and guided. There is a Power greater than we are, which provides guidance and bountifully supplies our every need. Jesus borrows from the analogy of Psalm 23: "The Lord is my shepherd. I shall not want..." We are to follow the Lord, the Law of God, and we will find that goodness, and mercy follow us all the days of our life, for we will dwell in the house of the Lord forever. It is in this way that the meek inherit the earth.

In the Will

If we ever intend to have a joyous, fulfilling experience of life we must come to the awareness that this is Gods will for us as well. God has already provided the abundance of Life. It is ours to accept. God's wisdom guides us to the point where we can see it clearly. We come into our inheritance to the degree that we recognize it, and choose to accept it. "Thy will be done" was Jesus's affirmation of acceptance. It affirms that the will of God is for our greatest good and well-being. It is the realization that we are blessed, by God, as we let the will of God be done for us and through us. What might that divine will be? For an infinite God, it can only be that Life be expressed fully and freely within you, through you, as you. Anything else would be in conflict with Its own nature. An accepting attitude, a calm reliance upon this unseen principle, never fails those who are meek enough to work with It.

THE RIGHTEOUS

> Blessed *are* they which do hunger and thirst after
> righteousness: for they shall be filled.
> Mt. 5:6

Fulfillment

This verse could be restated as: Blessed are the empty cups, for
they shall be filled. It is another instance where the wisdom of the
Psalms is restated: "my cup runneth over. Surely goodness and
mercy shall follow me all the days of my life." (Ps. 23:5-6) The
wisdom of such statements is that they make a pronouncement
predicated on a universal Truth, rather than facts and circumstance.
In this case, the premise is that of an infinite source that supplies
all, all the time; even in the shadow of death or the presence of
enemies, the Lord is my Shepherd (source). In an infinite universe,
there are no empty places or isolated spaces. The infinite God is
everywhere, and all that It has, all that It is, It gives. That is why
our cup is filled to overflowing. Of course, a horse can be led to
water, but not made to drink. In an abundant universe, no one is
force fed. Plenty of people go hungry, for many reasons; even so,
the cup of acceptance is always filled.

More is promised in this verse than mental and spiritual
fulfillment. It is easy to believe that those who seek righteousness
will have their mind filled with ideas, but what about their belly?
Does the philosopher get to eat? Shall we live on love? Jesus did
not live a life of sacrifice, but of fulfillment. He did not teach that
there is a physical life and a separate spiritual life, but one infinite
life. He taught that the kingdom of heaven is within us and that we
live in God's kingdom now. This verse is developed later in the
Sermon on the Mount where we are told not to worry over what we
shall eat and what we shall wear: "But seek ye first the kingdom of

God, and his righteousness; and all these things shall be added unto you." (Mt. 6:33)

Be Hungry

The blessed hunger for righteousness. Their blessing is not that they are hungry but that they do not settle for that which does not satisfy. They do not try to fill up their lives, but to fulfill their lives. Jesus expressed this hunger for righteousness when he said to his disciples: "I have meat to eat that ye know not of." They didn't understand, so he explained: "My meat is to do the will of him that sent me, and to finish his work." (Jn. 4:32-34) Many of us try to satisfy our hunger for fulfillment by filling up our bellies, and filling our days and nights with distractions, only to be hungry still. Those who are truly fulfilled are the ones who find fulfillment in their life's work, even if they have only their daily bread to eat. Their blessing is not that they hunger or thirst, but that they put first things first.

You can eat all you wish, but it will not be fulfilling, and you will just get fatter. Our hunger and thirst for righteousness must be satisfied first. It is a matter of prioritizing: letting ideas precede actions, knowing the Truth before you struggle to be free. If we work with the Law of Life, we will bring fulfillment into our lives rather than limitation. The reason most people find their lives to be an uphill struggle is that when they realize what they want, they immediately go after the things, conditions and circumstances they lack. At the outset, it seems reasonable to get a cup and fill it with water if you are thirsty, but it is not the most practical approach. Jesus taught: "Whosoever drinketh of this water shall thirst again: But whosoever drinketh of the water I shall give him shall never thirst:" (Jn.4:13-14) He was telling us to look to what we have within, and then we will at no time be in want again. When we try to have things, which are not rooted deep within us, they soon wither and fade, and we must go searching time and again, never fulfilled.

Satisfied

Fulfillment is not achieved by satisfying your appetite and getting your needs met. It is not an achievement or acquisition; it is a realization. Fulfillment is an inner awareness, but not to be confused with being full of yourself. You do not find fulfillment by satisfying, or not satisfying, your appetite; nor by getting or not getting your needs met. Fulfillment is not found in salvation; nor is it achieved through self-sacrifice. That path leads to self-righteousness and never being fulfilled. The righteous are blessed as they do more than enough to be satisfied. There may be an easier, cheaper, more expedient way to do things, but they continue to do the right thing in the right way. That is the only satisfactory way to do things, for anything less is not enough. They invest more of themselves for this is the only way to be fulfilled.

Although the blessed may suffer for righteousness sake, because they are willing to, they are not as willing to suffer fools and foolishness. The self-righteous man may feel satisfied with himself and his effort, but because he does not do enough, or does just enough, to satisfy his relationship with God and mankind, he remains unfulfilled. It is the sense of fulfillment that satisfies hunger and thirst and distinguishes the righteous from the self-righteous. The self-righteous man does what he deems to be right for himself, ignoring God and what is right for all, while the righteous man satisfies the requirements of the Law of God. By being true to Life's principles, the righteous man is true to himself and cannot then be false to any man. And what, you may wonder, are the requirements of the Law of God, which we must satisfy for righteousness sake and to know fulfillment in life?

- "The first of all the commandments is, Hear, O Israel; The Lord our God is one Lord: And thou shalt love the Lord thy God with

25

all thy heart, and with all thy soul, and with all thy mind, and with all thy strength: this *is* the first commandment. And the second *is* like, *namely* this, Thou shalt love thy neighbour as thyself. There is none other commandment greater than these." (Mk. 12:29-31)

Fulfillment is the embodiment and experience of righteousness. A right relationship with Life might be realized in abiding by the Law, following the Golden Rule, having a good attitude towards all men, and the ability to love in spite of the appearances. Having a vision in mind is essential, but it is not sufficient. Likewise, merely affirming the Truth is not enough; we must prove it. Conscious acts avail nothing until they are confirmed by our actions. A sincere conviction must result in actual commitment to the goodness of Life. Commit an act of courage, of love, generosity and mercy. Fulfillment is found in righteousness, for righteousness is realized in the way one lives, not the way one thinks.

- "Wherefore, by their fruits ye shall know them." (Mt. 7:20)

THE MERCIFUL

Blessed *are* the merciful: for they shall obtain mercy.
Mt. 5:7

A Principle of Life

In this verse, Jesus described a particular application of a fundamental principle of Life. It has been called the principle of Sowing and Reaping — Cause and Effect. Jesus taught that it shall be done unto as we believe and that as we give unto others so shall others give unto us. Ernest Holmes called it the Law of Correspondence, stating that the Law of Life responds to us by working through us, fulfilling our life to the level of our consciousness. Ralph Waldo Emerson called it the Law of Compensation, wherein our compensation is equal to our consciousness.

Mercy and Kindness

There have been many descriptions and analogies of this basic truth of life: We experience what we express. If we express mercy, we will experience mercy. If we express love, we will experience love. Jesus expanded on this verse in the parable of a king who called his servants to account. One servant owed more than he could repay, so he asked for mercy. The king was moved with compassion and forgave the debt. A short time later, that same servant showed no mercy to those who were indebted to him, demanding payment or imprisonment. When the king learned of this, he demanded full payment of the debt and showed no mercy to that servant. (See Mt.18:23-35)

The parable does not make the case for God responding kindly in one moment and unkindly the next, but of Life responding in kind as we change our mind. When the servant thought that mercy and forgiveness were acceptable responses to debt, he was forgiven. When the servant thought that mercy and forgiveness were out of the question, his own debt was mercilessly demanded of him. It would be a mistake to think that the king (God, Life) is fickle; it was the servant who changed his mind. The law of Life responds to us by corresponding to us. It can only do for us what It can do through us. When we are merciful, we experience Life in kindness. When we are no longer merciful, our experience of Life will have to be of some other kind.

Consciousness

Do not think that Life deals callously with the unmerciful. The truth of the matter is that they have dealt cruelly with themselves; for the way they view the world is also the way they view themselves. Whether or not they are conscious of this makes no difference. The lack of mercy for others makes for a merciless consciousness. Since they are not experiencing mercy within themselves, they do not know it and cannot expect it or accept it from others. They judge and condemn themselves with their attitude towards others.

Likewise, the man who is willing to forgive has established a consciousness of forgiveness, and the whole world responds with goodness and mercy towards him. Even so, we must remember that the Law responds to his inner feeling of mercy, not to any acts of kindness or charity he may perform. It can only work for us as It works through us. To do a kindness for someone so that they will help you, or to forgive someone because you feel you might lose their friendship if you don't, is neither merciful or forgiving. You will not get what you hoped for, but what you feared. You will reap the results of trying to use people; you will be used. And, fearing the loss of love; you will lose it.

The blessed are merciful, and they are compensated with mercy. Those who do not know mercy have not the consciousness of mercy and are in no position to receive mercy from others. Life

28

and the living relate to us in the way we relate to all. If we are merciful, we establish relationships that afford mercy to us as well as from us.

THE PURE IN HEART

Blessed *are* the pure in heart: for they shall see God.
Mt. 5:8

See God?

It was a radical suggestion! The ancient traditions forbid the notion of coming face to face with the LORD. You weren't supposed to say God's name or even write it, let alone look upon God. That would be too up close and personal for a distant deity, a God on the mountain or secluded in the Temple. The last man supposed to see God's face was Adam, and we know how bad things turned out in the garden. Not even Moses was granted the privilege of seeing God's face. When he asked to see the glory of God, the Lord said that he would show him goodness, graciousness, and mercy and tell him his name, but that would be the extent of their relationship. "Thou canst not see my face: for there shall no man see me, and live." (Ex. 33:19-20)

So what are we to make of that? Perhaps it expresses the idea that we can see what God does, but not what God is. It is invisible, intangible, spiritual — not a finite physical being but an infinite metaphysical Being. How can we possibly see God? Certainly not with the eyes, for all that the eye sees is the expression of God's life and but a small part at that. I believe in an infinite God, and I know that neither the farsighted nor the near-sighted can focus on infinity; nevertheless, even a blind man can see God! To see God is to understand God. It is reminiscent of what the Apostle Paul said of how our understanding of God would change when we perceive Its perfection (wholeness and completeness), and completely understand It:

- But when that which is perfect is come, then that which is in part shall be done away. When I was a child, I spake as a child, I understood as a child, I thought as a child; but when I became a man, I put away childish things. For now we see through a glass, darkly; but then face to face: now I know in part; but then shall I know even as I am known. (1 Cor. 13:10-12)

Paul speaks of a shift in consciousness from what we imagine God to be, to one where we know God in the same sense that God knows us. Then we will no longer have a partial knowledge, as a being apart from God, but a sense of oneness with God. Perhaps this is what it means to see God face to face. Facing up to something means to see it for what it is. Perhaps no man can see God's face and live because our humanity or our physical senses can't make sense of oneness with God. Physically, we appear separate, apart, even though spiritually we are one life and being. Seeing face to face is seeing one another for what we are.

So what are we to make of Jesus's statement that the pure in heart will see God? Do they not perceive God now? Was he only promising that they would see God after they died? Is a purity of heart a reserved seat in heaven or is it the consciousness that perceives God, here and now? Clearly, he was referring to those who have purity of heart right now; so the question becomes one of where they will see God, given that they have the consciousness to do so now.

Jesus often stated the obvious, in a way, that had profound implications: seek, and ye shall find; knock, and it shall be opened; sow and reap; give, and it shall be given unto you. Perhaps he was saying that if you can see God now, you'll see God then, as always. If you see God in others, or look upon others as God must see them (with purity of heart) and love them even as God loves them, then you will surely see God for you are already seeing from that divine perspective, that sense of perfect oneness.

Purity of Heart

If purity of heart is love, or if love purifies the heart (mind), then the pure of heart see God now. Those who love recognize the perfection of their loved ones. They perceive that which is perfect, whole and complete in the one they love. Is that not a perception of the presence and essence of God within and as their beloved? It reminds me of the scolding Jesus gave to the disciple Philip: "If ye had known me, ye should have known my Father also: and from henceforth ye know him, and have seen him." Philip saith unto him, "Lord, shew us the Father, and it sufficeth us." Jesus saith unto him, "Have I been so long time with you, and yet hast thou not known me, Philip? he that hath seen me hath seen the Father; and how sayest thou then, Shew us the Father? Believest thou not that I am in the Father, and the Father in me?" (Jn. 14:7-10)

Recognition

It could be that a loving perception is what Jesus was speaking about to Philip: To know me is to love me! To recognize someone is to see in them, what you already know of them. The pure in heart perceive God within, and, therefore, are able to recognize the presence and essence of God within all. That is seeing God face to face, on a personal scale. It is the perception of one another without any sense of separation. It is an act of recognition, an act of love. It is recognition of the perfection of Life, the infinite Being within us, as us.

Perhaps Jesus was referring to love as purity of heart, but even so, that too is a reference to the consciousness of heaven. Remember where Jesus located that spiritual realm: "… the kingdom of God is within you." (Lk. 17:20) Purity of heart (love) is the consciousness of being one with God — of being perfect, "… even as your Father which is in heaven is perfect." (Mt. 5:48) Where else might one expect to see God face to face, but within? Purity of heart is the consciousness of Heaven, and those who dwell in heaven most certainly see God.

Cause = Effect

This verse does not make a promise. It states the principle of cause and effect. Being pure in heart has the effect of knowing the presence of God within you. The cause (being) and the effect (knowing) are one and the same, and this is always the way it is. The purity Jesus spoke of was an innermost state, being of the heart. It is not a matter of doing good deeds, though this would result from inner purity. It is not even a case of thinking pure thoughts. It is a state of being in which one is aware of the love of God.

When we can clear away the limiting and confusing attitudes and fears that obscure our inner vision, we too will be able to see the divinity that indwells all. We will be pure in heart and know the love of God.

THE PEACEMAKERS

Blessed *are* the peacemakers; for they shall be called the children of God.

Mt. 5:9

Compromise and Conflict

We can think of peace, and, therefore, the role of peacemaker, in two ways: Firstly, we may consider peace to be Peace on Earth, an end of war and the cessation of mankind's conflicts. Secondly, we may think of peace as the inner consciousness which stills the conflict one has in mind. Is the peacemaker Jesus had in mind the one who strives to end the strife between two or more people, or the strife within oneself?

The first option is an extremely difficult task, and usually all that is accomplished is a compromise based upon self-interests and coercion. There is no peace in this, for a compromise does not replace the consciousness of strife and conflict. Throughout history, we can see that compromise has established cease-fires that led to retrenchment and rearmament, not peace. Hindsight shows that a compromise leads to being conflicted, and eventually to more conflicts. Compromise brings the promise of peace, but not peace.

The second option should be considered the first option; because if we were at peace within ourselves, there might be fewer conflicts, and no need to compromise ourselves for others. Seeking peace through treaties leads to compromise, but not peace of mind. If you compromise your principles and interests to acquire that which is favorable you may find contentment, but not peace of mind. Contentment is a compromise that you make with yourself. It is a promise you make to be satisfied with what you got through the compromise.

As with world peace, inner peace cannot be achieved by compromise. In order to reach a compromise, there must be two parties in conflict, each willing to give up something to gain something they can't achieve alone. That does not describe the state of an individual, and though some think that arguing with themselves counts for two aggrieved parties, it does not. It is a no-win situation that cannot be resolved peacefully.

Others think that their inner conflict is not with themselves, but with God. They imagine the conflict within themselves to be an argument with God. They intend to resolve this inner conflict through compromise, by striking a bargain, with God. The hope is that God will provide a peaceful existence if one promises to abide by Its Law. Any one of us could achieve that resolution if it were not for the belief that we are not one with, but at odds with, God and everyone else.

Children of God

Though we are within our rights to compromise ourselves, who in their right mind, would try to compromise God, or wish to have a compromised God? God doesn't compromise Itself, make promises, or accept promises, and the children of God should never compromise themselves in their efforts to live in peace.

Throughout the infinite universe, the nature of Life is principled. God never compromises Itself, Its nature or principles. God does not give up something to gain something else. The Infinite provides all, even though It gains nothing in return. The infinite is one, and It is at peace with Itself. The infinite God cannot be in conflict; even so, conflicts can occur within It. It cannot be compromised, even though compromises can be made within It. God makes no promises, even though we do.

Jesus attributes our experience of peace to our relationship with God, by asserting that those who make peace are considered to be the children of God. The children of God express God's nature in their lives. God's nature is peaceful, and we express it by being peaceful. The children of God make peace by agreeing quickly with their adversary, by turning the other cheek and going the extra mile. Their compensation for being so agreeable is to perceive God within and know oneself as a child of God. All it takes is a peaceful, loving heart, and the following instructions:

- "Agree with thine adversary quickly, whiles thou art in the way with him;" (Mt. 5:25)
- "Ye have heard that it hath been said, An eye for an eye, and a tooth for a tooth: But I say unto you that ye resist not evil: but whosoever shall smite thee on thy right cheek, turn to him the other also. And if any man will sue thee at the law, and take away thy coat, let him have *thy* cloke also. And whosoever shall compel thee to go a mile, go with him twain. Give to him that asketh thee, and from him that would borrow of thee turn not thou away." (Mt. 5:38-42)

Make Peace with Yourself

What Jesus advised may not resolve conflicts with others; nevertheless, it is good advice for those who desire peace of mind. Your primary adversary is yourself, not anyone and everyone else. You are the one best situated to do you harm. You are the one who has hurt you the most. Your mistakes have taken a greater toll on you than anything anyone else has ever done to you. You have denied yourself more than anyone has withheld from you. Your first adversary is yourself. It is not them; it is you with whom you must keep the peace.

You can be at peace with yourself by keeping the agreements you have made with yourself, and by not further compromising yourself. Jesus advised that to rise above conflict we must go beyond what is demanded of us, required of us, or forced from us. We live free of our inner resistance and resentments as we choose to do more than is necessary. We are compromised by doing only

36

that which others require. It is as one gives all they have to give and does all that they can do, that they find peace of mind. This approach does not lessen the demands made upon us or that which others require of us; it simply resolves the inner conflicts and compromises which keep one from being at peace.

Make Peace with Others

Even though, you are the true adversary, others may step into an adversarial role with you. When we are not at peace, we invite conflict. If you think that your adversary is that person who is arguing with you, competing with you or working against you, think again. He has agreed to be your sparring partner, and finding further agreement with him will require a greater compromise.

Between the two of you, the one who wants peace, the one most in want of peace, the one most lacking peace, will be the one who compromises the most. The one who is most at peace will be the one who is least compromised in agreeing to it. Only those who have peace can live at peace with others. They are the peacemakers, because they would be and do as God is and does. They deserve to be known as the children of our Father.

- "Ye have heard that it hath been said, Thou shalt love thy neighbour, and hate thine enemy. But I say unto you, Love your enemies, bless them that curse you, do good to them that hate you, and pray for them which dreadfully use you, and persecute you; That ye may be the children of your Father which is in heaven: for he maketh his sun to rise on the evil and on the good, and sendeth rain on the just and on the unjust. For if ye love them which love you, what reward have ye? do not even the publicans the same? And if ye salute your brethren only, what do ye more than others? do not even the publicans so?" (Mt. 5:43-47)

Consciousness of Peace

The peacemaker that Jesus spoke of is a man who ends strife within himself, within his mind and soul, by taking affirmative action with respect to all. The peacemaker accomplishes this inner peace by affirmative prayer, alone. Nothing you do with people or about the conditions of the world will ever bring you peace. However, your prayer is a definite mental activity that resolves your conflicts, anger and fear. What will it take for you to be at peace, to be and do as God is and does? To be this peaceful requires the consciousness of God; it requires being conscious of Perfection.

- "Be ye therefore perfect, even as your Father which is in heaven is perfect." (Mt. 5:48)

Peace of mind requires not only that you be perfect (whole and complete, not compromised) but that you recognize that state of wholeness and completeness in all. It requires that you respect all, even as God does. God gives of Itself freely and equally with respect to all. When our consciousness is clear, we will see as God sees. We will respect one another for we are all one with the Father of all.

Agreement

If you wish to be at peace, then agree quickly, with yourself while you still can. Agree within, before you begin to play the role of Devil's advocate. Sustain that inner accord where, instead of struggling between two points of view, you are of one mind with God. Be at peace, and others may find you to be agreeable.

If you wish to make peace with others, be agreeable, but don't agree with them or give your consent to them. You need not be argumentative, judgmental and antagonistic, but, neither do you need to make agreements you cannot keep with yourself, and by yourself. Be open-minded and respectful of another's perspective but align yourself with Life, and in so doing you will be true to yourself and right with the world.

If it is too late for that — if you are feeling defensive and your words are offensive, divisive and argumentative, then you must give your consent: realign your thoughts and feelings by agreeing with that which is pleasing and of good will. Be gracious, and thankful, accepting that which is to your liking.

Do not confuse giving your consent with surrender. Consent is not a "sweet surrender" to an over-powering deity that knows and wants what is best for us. We need only surrender to an over-whelming force that is opposed to us. Fortunately, when it comes to a contest of wills, there is no such force opposed to us. When it comes to living our life, there is no one and nothing to surrender to. There are people who would control us, but that requires our agreement and cooperation. Free will is a quality that we cannot surrender. Our consent cannot be taken from us; we must give it, or it is not consent.

The will of God cannot be forced upon us. When our will is in agreement with God, that is when our will is of God. When our will is in alignment with God's will, then they are one and the same. Then, Thy will may be done. To achieve such alignment requires our consent. Don't hold your breath while waiting for God to agree with you! To consent to God's will is to choose to be in agreement with God. It is to choose to do and be as God is and does. For the will of God to be done in our life we must do it. We must be in agreement with It and give our consent to It. Obviously, God's will has not been forced upon us. That is not because God is powerless, but because there is no such thing as the will of God for us. God's will may be done through us, but that requires our agreement and consent. If you would be at peace, give your consent and agreement to that which is in alignment with Life, for that will be to your liking and of greatest benefit to you.

THE PERSECUTED

Blessed *are* they which are persecuted for righteousness sake;
for theirs is the kingdom of heaven.

Mt. 5:10

Right and Wrong

I find it very difficult to distinguish between the righteous and
the self-righteous. I don't know how they tell themselves apart!
Most of us strive to be right, do right and choose rightly, but how
are we to determine what is right?

I thought that the distinction between a correct choice and a
morally right choice, might make it easier; but the morality police
consider the only correct choice to be the morally right choice. I
wondered if the distinction between that which is legal and that
which is morally right might suffice, but no; we are to believe that
the correct and legal choice is not necessarily the right choice. It
seems the morally right are determined to re-write the laws, or
break them!

I've wondered where free choice comes into these deliberations.
Philosophers of morality have written that if one does the right
thing for the wrong reason, then he is wrong; and if one does the
wrong thing for the right reasons, then he is right. This logic leads
to the conclusion that to be right one need only do that which is
reasonable; but who determines what is reasonable? If it is the one
doing the reasoning, are we not back to self-righteousness?

Consider the self-sacrificing, who freely choose to suffer so that
others will not suffer. They seem to think it incorrect, illegal, or
morally wrong for others to suffer, but they believe they suffer
righteously — for the morally right reasons. Does this mean that
the self-sacrificing are also self-righteous? Does it mean that self-
sacrifice is righteous suffering, but the suffering of any others, for

any other reasons (i.e., suffering the consequences, accepting the inevitable, putting up with the weather) is just not right?

It appears to me that if you decide for yourself what is right, then you can't be right — only self-righteous. To avoid this, there must be an external, impersonal standard which establishes the right thing to think and do. But there are many standards by which people determine what is right, and this results in everyone making what they believe to be the right choice; and almost everyone else believing they are wrong. It is even more difficult to determine who is more self-righteous: those who determine what is right for themselves, or those who judge them to be wrong.

Hypocrisy

I also find it difficult to distinguish between the self-righteous and the hypocritical. Like the judgmental, who pretend at righteousness and achieve only self-righteousness, the hypocrite as well plays the part of a righteous man. The sole distinction I am aware of is that the hypocrite puts on an act in public, while the self-righteous continues that public personna in private. Jesus denounced as hypocrites those who ignore a fault in their own perception while pointing it out in others. Jesus warned us of self-righteousness and hypocrisy when he said: "Judge not, that ye be not judged. ... And why behold the mote that is in thy brothers eye and considerst not the beam that is in thine own eye? ... ... Thou hypocrite, ..." (Mt. 7:1-5)

Some think they avoid being hypocritical and self-righteous by judging themselves and everyone else impartially, but they miss the point. Righteousness is not a question of whether you are right or not in the views you hold of yourself and others. It is a question of whether or not you judge. To avoid being self-righteous, we must refrain from judging anyone by any standard.

Righteousness

Jesus understood what was required to be a principled person, for as a rabbi, he would have been well acquainted with the Book of Psalms, which begins with a description of the righteous man:

Blessed is the man that walketh not in the counsel of the ungodly, nor standeth in the way of sinners, nor sitteth in the seat of the scornful. But his delight is in the law of the LORD; and in his law doth he meditate day and night. And he shall be like a tree planted by the rivers of water, that bringeth forth his fruit in his season; his leaf also shall not wither; and whatsoever he doeth shall prosper. The ungodly are not so: but are like the chaff which the wind driveth away. Therefore the ungodly shall not stand in the judgment, nor sinners in the congregation of the righteous. For the LORD knoweth the way of the righteous: but the way of the ungodly shall perish. (Ps. 1)

In New Thought parlance, righteous is understood as right-use of the Law. A righteous person remains committed to the law of the Lord, even though he is persecuted for his principles. Life works, and the way it works is Law. A righteous person is one who works with this Law of Life.

We all desire to lead a principled life, but none of us wish to be persecuted for it: no sane person would. Note that in the Sermon on the Mount, Jesus did not say a righteous person would be persecuted, but that if we are persecuted in spite of living a principled life, and if we continue to live righteously, we will be blessed. Only a fool would forsake principles that work because he is being ridiculed or rejected by those who try in vain to make their lives work.

Persecuted / Prosecuted

When the focus is on you, it may be difficult for you to know whether you are being persecuted or prosecuted. If it is because of your beliefs, then you are being persecuted. If it is because you have committed a crime, you are being prosecuted. If you are working within the law, you can't be prosecuted, only persecuted. If you are breaking the law, you can be prosecuted.

Being persecuted, not prosecuted, is a sign that you are doing what works: working within the law. Law-breakers can be prosecuted. The righteous may be persecuted. Take heart if you are persecuted for righteousness sake: you are among good company. All those who have expanded our awareness of Truth were persecuted, ridiculed, rejected and ignored. However, take care: those whose beliefs are not true are also persecuted. Being persecuted is not proof of being right. It only indicates that you have a new thought, not that it is true. The righteous are not blessed because they are persecuted, but because they are righteous! Their blessing is inherent in working with the Law. They are doing what works in Life, and will have the blessings of working with Life.

Steadfast

Suffering for righteousness sake is not a sacrifice; it is perseverance and patience. To suffer means to continue; and to suffer righteously is to continue working with the Law. The discomfort we suffer, which can occur even when you are engaged in a right use of spiritual principles, is resistance to change. As we become more aware, it may be difficult to let go of old patterns of thought. They are familiar, and we would stay with them if we could. In this confused state of mind, problems may arise, which persecute you. Nevertheless, remain steadfast with the Law, and It will see you clear and your awareness will be of the kingdom of Heaven. This is the promise which Jesus made. Let us believe it and know that nothing stands in our way but our fears of the new day, our clinging to the security of a limited past. And nothing can free us but our consistent and determined mental work with God's Law.

43

THE LORD'S PRAYER
Mt. 6:9-13

Our Father which art in heaven,

Hallowed be thy name.

Thy kingdom come.

Thy will be done in earth as *it is* in heaven.

Give us this day our daily bread.

And forgive us our debts, as we forgive our debtors.

And lead us not into temptation, but deliver us from evil:

For thine is the kingdom, and the power, and the glory, for ever.

Amen.

Instruction

> After this manner therefore pray ye:
> Mt. 6:9

The Lord's Prayer is not a prayer. Jesus did not speak it as a prayer, but shared it as instructions on how to pray, along with instructions on other spiritual disciplines. In Matthew 6:1-4, we find instructions on charitable giving, followed by instruction on prayer in verses 5 - 8, with an example of the way to pray in verses 9 - 13. These verses are followed by instruction on forgiveness in verses 14 - 15, fasting in verses 16 - 18 and setting spiritual priorities in verses 19 - 24.

Some take his instructions to mean that one is to repeat the words Jesus spoke as their own prayer, reciting it in all circumstances where prayer is called for. Such a literal understanding is tantamount to pushing clothing aside to "enter into thy closet and when thou hast shut thy door, pray to thy Father which is in secret;" (Mt. 6:6) I don't believe Jesus wanted his followers to rely on his faith rather than their own, or to use his words rather than their own. Jesus taught how to think, not what to say. He taught that prayer was a silent communion. He taught that we should not use vain repetitions. How ironic that the most often repeated prayer in the history of mankind is attributed to him.

Teaching people to repeat the thoughts of another is easier than teaching them to think for themselves. We teach children to memorize the multiplication tables because it is easier than teaching the principle of multiplication, and it supplies the answers commonly needed. The memorization of answers is intended as a device for keeping ones focus on the true until they have an understanding of the truth. Sadly repetition and recitation has become an expedient replacement for inspiration and understanding. O ye of little faith!

OUR FATHER

Our Father which art in heaven, Hallowed be thy name.
Mt. 6:9

Christ Consciousness

There is no other statement in the teachings of Jesus that says as much as "Our Father". These two words expand our awareness of the infinite nature of God and summarize our relationship with It. These words represent, and we tend to ignore the fact that Jesus' teachings promoted, a radical departure from the orthodox view of God and man. This is because we've been taught to recite prayers without understanding what they mean. We've been taught to repeat words, rather than be inspired by them. It has been suggested by some religious disciplines that if one repeats a prayer, an affirmation, a mantra, enough times they will one day be inspired. It is possible, but it is also likely that the repetition will lull the mind to unconsciousness before they are lucky enough to have a flash of insight. Let us awaken that which slumbers: the consciousness of the Christ.

One Father

Jesus didn't say that we should pray to his Father, but to our Father. Much has been said, and many misled, by overlooking this one point: the relationship that Jesus had with God is the same relationship we have with God. Whether we know it or not, whether we are conscious of it or not, whether we express and experience it or not, we are as close to God as Jesus was. Obviously, Jesus realized this, and we would be better off if we did as well.

We are all the same in nature, and I don't refer to our human nature, but to our spiritual nature. If we wish to think of Jesus as divine, then we have to think of ourselves as divine. If we think of ourselves as divine, then we must realize that everyone is divine. The basis for claiming our divinity is what we believe about God, not what we think about ourselves. If we think of God as infinite (Review Mk. 12:28-34) then we must realize that It is one, and we are one with It (Review Jn. 10:30) No one can be separate from the infinite One. If the spirit of Life is infinite, then our life and spirit is infinite as well, for there can be only one infinite spirit, one infinite life, one infinite being and each one of us an individualization of It. Jesus told his disciples that if you truly know someone, then you should also know the One. We should be able to recognize the Father in the child, and the child in the Father, for they are of one and the same nature.

While most religions present the notion of God as separate from the world and mankind, Jesus taught that the kingdom of God is within us. (Read Lk. 17:21) This begins to make sense if you think of yourself as a spiritual being rather than a physical body; and if you accept the premise of an infinite, singular, universal God. In an infinite universe, the Universal is within the individual, and the individual is within the Universal. Jesus said: "I and *my* Father are one." (Jn. 10:30) He was not proclaiming that he was God but that he was inseparable from the infinite God. Jesus taught that the Father is within us and that we are within the Father. (Review Jn. 10:31-39) He did not deny the physical, but uplifted it, thus uplifting our self-concept to a level of reverence and respect. He was proclaiming our spiritual nature as he claimed his own, and the basis of his claim was this belief in the Infinite Being.

The traditional concept was that our ancestors are our fathers and that we are nothing more than flesh and bone. Jesus claimed that God is our Father and that we are much more than flesh and bone. To claim God as your Father is to affirm that you too are a spiritual being. It is the realization that God is not just our creator or our provider; It is our life. To think of God as our Father is to consider It to be our very source and essence, our life and being. It is to affirm our oneness with the infinite life of God.

Though most students of religion concern themselves with defending claims about Jesus, his own claim to be a child of God says something more about God than it does about himself. It speaks to a loving relationship, not a judgmental or controlling relationship. Anyone who has children knows that you have to love them, and you can't control them. Contrast this with the idea that God is our judge, or our king. Jesus didn't believe in a God that ruled over us. It is evident from his effort to teach, and his mission to fulfill prophecies, that he believed we can know the will of God and we can choose or refuse to do as God wills. Again, it is a loving parental relationship. It is a relationship of freedom — of choice and consequence. It is not a favored relationship, but a principled relationship; and yet still a loving relationship. Love gives and forgives, again and again, constantly; for that is the nature of love and love is the nature of our relationship with God, our Father.

Hallowed Name

Whatever we say when we call upon God, when we rely upon Its nature and put our faith in Its Law, that statement tends to become our name for it. What we say of It defines our use of It, our knowledge and awareness of It, but our name for It can't begin to describe Its infinite being.

Thus, our name for our God says more about us than God. Jesus referred to God as Father because he considered himself to be a child of God, a spiritual being. Well, in fact, the word we translate as Father is more accurately translated as Papa, designating a more loving and less formal relationship than we ascribe to a father figure.

The word 'god' is not a name, even though we use it as such and capitalize it as if it were a name. A god is whatever we call upon or try to invoke in our prayer. As the story is told in Exodus 3:13-15, Moses asked to know the name of God. The response was "I AM THAT I AM". For lack of a better name, I AM is the name we are to use when calling upon God.

God doesn't have a name; It has an infinite nature. I AM is not a name; it is a statement of Its being, Its infinite nature. Trying to define the infinite by adding another word to the statement, putting a name to It, would only serve to limit It. We can't do that to God. We can't name God. We can only name, and limit our awareness of God, and ourselves. We set limits on our self-concept by completing the statement: "I am ..." It does not matter what we say, for, however, we define ourselves will be a limited description of our infinite potential. This can be useful, necessary and expedient. It can even be creative, but it is not what we would do if the name of God were hallowed.

"Hallowed be thy name." This is a statement that affirms our intention to be aware of and express the wholeness of God, not a partial perception. For the name of God to be hallowed it must be treated as holy, revered and respected when used. We usually don't do that. We do not hallow the name of God when we make statements like: I am so sick and tired of ... I am unhappy. I am mad. If we would hallow the name of God, then our statement of our being would be a statement that we know (or believe) to be true of God as well. I am loving. I am at peace. I am whole and complete: perfect. I am in harmony. I am abundant. I am intelligent.

When we don't think or feel so divinely inspired, then instead of making some statement that demeans God as well as ourselves, we should just say: I don't think I can. I don't feel good. I feel bad, sad, unhappy. If we more accurately and correctly stated the issue, we'd be better able to resolve it. The problem is never what we are, and usually what we think and feel.

49

THE KINGDOM OF GOD

> Thy kingdom come. Thy will be done in earth as *it is* in heaven.
> Mt. 6:10

A Matter of Time

At the time, many who heard Jesus preach about the kingdom of God hoped he was referring to a resurgence of the kingdom of Israel, which had been conquered many times by other kingdoms and was currently under the rule of the Roman Empire. But Jesus was speaking of a spiritual state, not a geopolitical kingdom. Other leaders had been hailed as the messiah because of their willingness to rebel against Roman rule, but Jesus sought to fulfill the prophecies of the messiah through prayer, repentance, teaching and healing. His teachings challenged the orthodox view of God and were considered heresy, but it was for sedition that he was crucified. By equating the kingdom of God with the kingdom of Israel, his statements and claims were taken as a challenge to Roman authority, instead of what they were: a challenge to the religious authorities of his day.

We now have the benefit of hindsight and thousands of years of preaching and teaching that draw the distinction clearly between Israel and Gods kingdom. But still, confusion persists. People still insist that Jesus was speaking of the kingdom to come, someday, on earth, with either God or Jesus himself ruling like a king. They still ask when the prophecies will be fulfilled, rather than how they are to be fulfilled. They still think that establishing the kingdom of God is only a matter of time, and like those of old, they will be disappointed.

Jesus' teachings about the kingdom of God can only be fulfilled personally and spiritually; prophecies about Israel, only politically and militarily. If that is not obvious, then perhaps a corollary will clarify: Jesus' teachings about the kingdom of God cannot be fulfilled politically or militarily; and prophecies about the kingdom of Israel cannot be fulfilled personally and spiritually.

The Pharisees and many of Jesus' followers were confused about the nature of the kingdom of God; but Jesus was not confused. Jesus did not believe in the kingdom of prophecy; he believed in the kingdom of God. He did not believe it was just a matter of time; he believed it was now. It would be good for his followers to catch up to where he stood on the question of when, where and how God's kingdom is to come: And when he was demanded of the Pharisees, when the kingdom of God should come, he answered them and said, "The kingdom of God cometh not with observation: "Neither shall they say, Lo here! or, lo there! for, behold, the kingdom of God is within you." (Lk.17:20-21)

The only way in which that which is within us can ever come forth is for it to be expressed, and thereby manifestly experienced in our life. It is a matter of spiritual awareness and self-expression. I think we owe it to Jesus and to ourselves, to not perpetuate or participate in a belief that the kingdom of God has been postponed, or that we must wait for it to come. To pray Thy kingdom come, is to pray for it to come forth from within us; and that is not a question of when, but of how.

The Will of God

When Jesus spoke of God's kingdom, he was talking about the spiritual state of living in harmony with God's law. The kingdom of God is the realm of God's Law, and it stretches as far and wide as we abide by that Law. For it to come forth we must behold it within us, embrace it consciously, and embody it by being an expression of it. We must live according to those spiritual principles that undergird all man-made laws. I believe in the kingdom of God because I believe in the will of God being done. I believe that the kingdom of God comes forth as the will of God is

51

done — on earth as in heaven. I believe that the kingdom of God can come but only as it comes forth in our thought and deed, establishing harmony between what we believe, what we do unto others, and what is done unto us. I believe the kingdom of God is within us, and we must behold it in mind in order for it to be brought forth in our world.

What might the will of God be? Whatever it is, it is universal and not personal. It is Law. The will of God is to be found in the way God works, and it can be understood as universal principles. Jesus taught that it is the will of God that:

- We have life more abundantly. (See Jn.10:10)
- We shouldn't worry because it is the Father's pleasure to give us the kingdom. (Read Lk.12:32)
- We inherit that which is inherent: the kingdom of God. (Review Mt.19:29)

The will of God is that it be done unto us as we believe, that we receive as we give, and that we reap more than we sow.

A GIVEN

Give us this day our daily bread.
Mt. 6:11

A Demand?

The words we use in prayer establish an attitude, an approach to
Life. New Thought teachings on prayer emphasize the importance
of being affirmative and accepting as we turn within to pray. Our
prayers are not begging, bargaining, beseeching requests. We are
careful to use words that affirm and express the qualities of Life
we desire to experience; for the way we turn to It is the way it will
turn out. Our attitude going in will determine what we get out. Our
purpose in prayer is to establish an attitude of gratitude, the
grateful acceptance of the gracious gifts of life, which have already
been given.

While it is true that our prayers need not ask God for anything,
it is a mistake to think we are in a position to make demands upon
Life. It is a mistake to think that if we are not asking, we must be
telling: give me what I ask for; give me my bread; give me what I
want. Prayer is not an opportunity to tell God what to do, or what
to be. Praying for God to be good to you, to give and to forgive
you, is a waste of time for that is already the nature of your
relationship with God. If you pray to remind yourself of your
blessings, then that is time well invested, but don't waste your time
asking for what is already given. Remember: all is given. God does
not withhold, or wait to be told to give. God gives first, and
foremost. It is Its nature to give of Itself constantly, continually,
and completely. Requests are unnecessary, and demanding is as
much a request as begging and pleading. If our words are
demanding because we have ignored all that is a given in life, then
our approach is more likely to result in self-reproach, blame and
rebuke than in receipt of a blessing. I can well imagine the

response I would get (no response at all) to a demand for bread: give me my bread! I might as well slam my fist on the table and wait for the bread to jump up and run to me, for all the good demanding will do for me. However, Jesus didn't suggest that I pray for my bread. His advice was that when I pray I affirm the idea that God gives us our bread every day. There is a definite adjustment to our attitude when we stop focusing on the individual and turn our attention to the universal. When we shift our focus from the needs of an individual to the creative processes that are universal, we are moving in the right direction.

A Command?

Our demands are nothing more than impolite requests; not to be confused with a command, which is a directive spoken with authority. In New Thought, prayer is thought of as an opportunity to provide direction to the expression of our life. Our prayer becomes more commanding as it is less demanding. A demand is only a plea made in a forceful way; though, no matter how loudly we speak, our demands do not have the force necessary to sway the universe from its course. A command, on the other hand, provides a course or channel, a means through which the creative power of Life may flow through us, in order to work for us. The captain of a sailing ship does not wait, or pray, for the winds to blow in the direction he would like to go. He gives thanks for the winds, and by the set of his sails and his command of the tiller they propel his ship to the destination of his choosing. He is not a commander of winds and waves, but of the ship he sails in.

Our command of prayer is often likened to the principle of sowing and reaping. Though a universal power is without equal, we may think of It as a passive, receptive, creative medium (like soil) which does not work for us until we make use it. New Thought preachers are fond of saying that a seed makes a demand upon the soil, and likewise, that our thought makes a demand upon the Soul of the Universe; which could be a workable analogy, if not for the fact that a demand gives nothing, but the empty expectation of what we want, and the hope that we will get it. A demand is a statement of what I expect of another, not what I accept of myself and for myself. A demand affirms only that I don't think I have it within me to do or be, or give as I would like to receive. I make no demands upon Life. I do not ask; I give, and as I give, the ways and means are established through which it is given to me, done unto me, and works for me. By my word (thought, self-concept, attitude, prayer), I command the expression of Life within and through me, as me. My word is as a seed of thought through which the universal force of Life is defined, refined and rendered into the particular form I choose to express and experience. My command is not an order, but an awareness that provides order and priority in the affairs of my life. My prayer is not an order issued to God, but an awareness that prioritizes and provides order to an otherwise chaotic thought process. When I am in command of my faculties I make no demands; I make choices and decisions.

People who think that they are in control can be very demanding. People who think they are in control of Life make demands upon It. Perhaps they think that by being demanding, they gain control. It reminds me of the demand that the prodigal son made.

- A certain man had two sons: And the younger of them said to his father, Father, give me the portion of goods that falleth to me. And he divided unto them his living. (Lk.15:11-12)

The prodigal son made a demand of his Father, and some think that the Lord's prayer advises us to make a similar demand: give us this day our daily bread. Some would call the prodigal son's demand an example of the power of prayer because he got what he wanted. It is even more impressive when you consider that the younger son was not entitled to any inheritance. His older brother was first in line to inherit his Fathers goods. Even so, the younger one got what he thought he deserved. His approach was demanding, and his life became demanding. His approach resulted in reproach, a rebuke: he got what he thought was owed to him. His demand was not ignored. Nothing was taken from him. He got what he was asking for, no less and no more.

Making demands never turns out as well as it seems at first. He got what he was asking for, but he settled for only a fraction of what was available. He turned his back on all his Father had to offer, and when hard times came, the young son was destitute. No matter how much you amass, a finite amount is soon diminished if not replenished from an infinite source. He would have been better off to continue to dwell within his Fathers house; something he eventually figured out when he considered his situation and came to himself. Eventually, we must all come to realize that the only demand that Life honors is the demand that It continues to be and do as It has always been, while we do what we will. So It is, and so it shall be.

A Plea for Charity?

We are told to pray for our "daily bread," yet we are not told what that is. Very few think that daily bread is bread, or only bread. It would be a severely limited and limiting God that kept you alive by providing only bread. Most expand the concept of bread to represent all that is necessary to sustain life, but then they limit how much one can have to only one days worth. An orthodox interpretation of this verse is that we are to pray for just enough to meet the needs of the day: our daily bread. If you would like to have more than that, you'll have to serve yourself. This interpretation lends credence to the notion that those who have more than they need must be self-serving, while the needy rely on God's care. With this in mind, it is easy to believe that those who live day to day are following the teachings of Jesus, and those who live an abundant life are not. Though, it is difficult to say who is more self-righteous: the self-serving, or those who think themselves to be the ones in God's care.

To better understand this verse I think we must consider it in the context of what Jesus taught, and what he was taught, about having enough. When considered on its own, this verse seems to suggest that one should pray for only as much as they need: a daily ration of bread. This practice of turning to God for our daily bread dates back to the time of Moses, when the Israelites wandered forty years in the desert. Moses told his followers that each morning God would provide a substance that they could use to make their daily bread. They referred to it as manna from heaven, because they didn't know what it was. Moses was admonishing his followers to stop worrying and approach each day with faith, knowing that God provides the stuff and substance that sustains us.

Moses also cautioned against greed and hoarding, telling his followers that they had to gather up the manna each morning, and use all they had that day, for manna couldn't be preserved or held in reserve. It is on this point that confusion, or a difference of opinion, rests. I think that Moses was instituting a daily discipline of turning to God as our source. That is what defined the manna in the wilderness as daily bread. However, a days worth of anything could be viewed as a limited supply, rather than a continuous supply. One could think of our daily bread as a survivalists diet of bread and water, but that is not what it represents. A careful reading of the experience of manna in the desert reveals that there was more than enough for everyone to have all they could gather. The substance of our daily bread is not in short supply. It is not a scarce commodity. We may make scarce use of the infinite resources available to us, but it would be a mistake to think that there isn't more than enough every day.

The Bread of Life

Praying for just enough to break even, to meet your needs, makes prayer a last resort, the refuge of those who hunger and thirst constantly for more. If one only gets enough for the day, they must pray tomorrow, and again the next day, and the next just to get by for another day. By meeting the need, instead of exceeding the need, charitable and 'need-based' systems of relief perpetuate a problem. They keep you hungry and coming back for more. If one understands what daily bread is, it becomes clear that the Lord's Prayer does not teach us to demand more or settle for less. That was not the approach to life that Jesus took, and it was not what he taught: "I am come that they might have life and that they might have *it* more abundantly." (Jn. 10:10)

We may not know what it is or how it is provided, but we should realize that God is the source of our supply -- our daily bread. And, if one traces the origin, the source of this manna from heaven, back to God, then even though we don't know quite what it is, we must admit that it is fundamentally of the same nature and quality as its source. The manna, or daily bread, is spiritual in nature. To pray for our daily bread is to seek the awareness that will sustain and bless us throughout the day. It is no wonder that Jesus said: "I am the bread of life." (Jn. 6:35) He considered himself to be spiritual in nature. He considered himself to be the Christ, a spiritual being. He identified himself with God, and he considered "living bread which came down from heaven" to be the spirit of God. (See Jn. 6:51) When Jesus teaches us to pray for our daily bread, he isn't talking about bread at all. Our daily bread is the awareness of the presence and essence of God, within and around us, every day. That is what sustains, and fulfills us.

RETRIBUTION

And forgive us our debts, as we forgive our debtors.
Mt. 6:12

Generosity

The accepted means of dealing with debt — retribution: an eye
for an eye and a tooth for a tooth. Repayment in kind was the way
to even the score and be able to relate as equals. Jesus' advised that
instead of just meeting the demands made upon us, we go beyond,
way beyond, what is required of us. (See Mt.5:39-42) If a person
demanded your coat, you should give it to him, and your cloak as
well. If you were expected to carry the load for a mile, carry it for
two miles. Instead of just meeting a request, just fulfilling an order,
just filling a bushel basket — fill everything to overflowing.
Instead of bartering with people for an equal exchange of goods,
draw upon a greater source to fill your measure, and their cup, to
overflowing. "Give, and it shall be given unto you; good measure,
pressed down, and shaken together, and running over, shall men
give into your bosom. For with the same measure that ye mete
withal it shall be measured to you again." (Lk.6:38)

The fundamental premise is that we apply the same limits, the
same rules, rulers and measures to everyone, including ourselves.
The measuring cup by which you give to others is the cup of your
acceptance. For your cup to be full to overflowing, you must be
using it to provide a heaping measure of goods to another. Only
then can you proclaim with the Psalmist: "My cup runneth over.
Surely goodness and mercy shall follow me all the days of my life:
and I will dwell in the house of the Lord forever." (Ps.23:5-6)

Divine Retribution

When debtors cannot repay your generosity, remember that
people are not your source. God is your source, but you have to

learn how to work with It in a way that prospers you. When a person cannot repay their debt to you, forgive it; thereby putting the Universe in your debt.

We have to learn how to give as It gives: freely, fully, abundantly. Being infinite, It gives first and foremost. It gives and forgives. It gives completely, and that is what it means to forgive — to give completely. As we give according to Its nature and principles, It gives through us, and we receive according to the very nature and principles by which we give. That is the way it works with giving, and with forgiving. We receive as we give; and we are forgiven as we forgive. If we forgive others their debt to us (reestablishing the relationship of equality by giving without expectation of repayment) then we are able to realize and accept that God also gives to us without expectation of repayment. We benefit from Life's blessings because it is Its nature to give more than we ask for, more than we can hold, and more than we can ever repay.

Forgiveness

Jesus said: "Judge not, and ye shall not be judged: condemn not, and ye shall not be condemned: forgive, and ye shall be forgiven:" (Lk. 6:37) When we realize forgiveness in our relationship with others, we realize that we too have been forgiven. We realize that we are still one with God: a relationship of equality in spirit and principle, though not in degree. It is obvious that a mouse and an elephant are not equal in size, but they are equally alive. The spirit of Life is infinite and does not admit to degrees. It gives all that It is, and we cannot begin to repay that debt, except by giving all that we have to give. We cannot give anything back to Life, but we can give what we have to give to the living.

We forgive others because we know we have been forgiven. When we have the consciousness of forgiveness, we say to those

who think they are in our debt, forget about it! There is more where that came from.
- When we forgive, we affirm abundance.
- When we forgive, we affirm our giving and our receiving.
- When we forgive, we affirm that we are forgiven.

By forgiving we affirm that we are not keeping score, and we are not trying to get even, because we are equals. Forgiveness confirms that we are one. The concept of an infinite establishes a realization of oneness which is the basis of relating as equals: we are all one.

No Debt / No Trespass

If we can relate to the infinite God as the one and only Father of us all, then we ought to consider relating to others as our equals. Consider this: if I am one with God, and you are one with God, then we are one with one another. In whatever sense we are one with God, in that sense, we are one with all that is one with God. The infinite nature of the one Father makes us one with everyone; and it is that oneness that is the basis for a sense of equality that cancels indebtedness. There can be no debt or debtor in a relationship where there is only One.

Ralph Waldo Emerson wrote in his essay on Gifts: "When the waters are at level, then my goods pass to him, and his to me. All his are mine, all mine his." He was making an analogy of the waters of a river, which when made level by a system of locks and damns, allows for the flow of goods upstream as well as down. It is as true of the waters of Life in which we are all immersed. When we are able to relate as equals, there is a level at which our goods flow freely to one another; for we are one and we know it. There are no debts or indebtedness between us when we relate as one; there is only giving and forgiving.

The verses which follow the Lord's Prayer describe forgiving debt as forgiving a trespass.

- "For if ye forgive men their trespasses, your heavenly Father
  will also forgive you: But if ye forgive not men their trespasses,
  neither will your Father forgive your trespasses." (Mt. 6:14-15)
The debt that is to be forgiven is not money borrowed; it is an act
of trespass. To trespass is to go beyond the bounds of propriety and
lawfulness; it is crossing the line. Trespass crosses the boundary of
another's personal space, violating their rights as an individual. We
trespass by crossing a line that separates one from another; but it is
not possible to trespass where there is no separation. It is not
possible to trespass against an infinite God, for there is no
separation between the infinite One and any one of us. But we
have a sense of separation within us: a belief, a perception, that we
are distant and apart; and we relate to one another as separate
individuals.

    Whether it is thought to be intentional or unintentional, the acts
of others can be seen as a violation, a trespass. Knowingly or
unknowingly we infringe on the rights of others. We can trespass
against them, or they against us. How is this to be forgiven?
Biblical law specifies restitution, penalties, fines, etc., as soon as
there is an acknowledgment of guilt. While retribution is ritualized
in the hope of clearing the conscience of the guilty and bringing
peace of mind to the aggrieved, it really amounts to a system of
inadequate punishments and payments: no one feels that they have
been made whole by an act of retribution. The only way to
alleviate trespass is to eliminate that which separates us: ignorance,
arrogance, schisms and isms, faults and other lies and lines that
define the separation between us.

    If the infinite God is our Father, then we do not trespass when
we enter into our Father's house, and we'll find no trespassers
therein. That house is infinite, so we never leave it or enter it; we
just have to realize that we're all in it together. Only love removes
the boundaries that define us and the faults that separate us from
everyone. Our loved ones do not trespass when they enter our

house. Our loved ones do not cross the line with us, for there is no line between us when we love God with all our heart, soul, and mind and love our neighbor as our self. (Review Mt. 22:36-40)

TEMPTATION

And lead us not into temptation, but deliver us from evil: For
thine is the kingdom, and the power, and the glory, for ever.
Amen.

Mt. 6:13

Don't tempt me!

It seems strange to think that God would tempt us. But perhaps
it is not so strange to those who remember the story of Job, an
exceedingly righteous man who was sorely tempted to curse God.
As the story goes, God allowed Satan to take all that Job held dear,
just to prove that Job would remain "... a perfect and an upright
man, one that feareth God, and escheweth evil." (Job 1:8)

Satan also provoked King David to take a census, a crime for
which God punished all of Israel. (See 1Ch. 21) Satan is mentioned
a few times in the Old Testament as the proponent of the evil
alternative, and we can find Satan mentioned prominently in the
Gospels. After Jesus fasted forty days in the wilderness, "... the
tempter came to him ..." suggesting that he try to turn stones into
bread, or try to fly instead of fall, or rule the kingdoms of the
world. Tempting offers, but Jesus' reply was: "Get thee hence,
Satan." (Mt.4:10) The next time Jesus spoke those words, it was in
response to his disciple Peter, who suggested that they get out of
town prior to the crucifixion. (See Mt.16:23) The Gospels attribute
even the betrayal of Jesus by Judas to the influence of Satan. (Read
Jn.13:27)

Don't believe it!

I don't believe Jesus thought that Peter was Satan in disguise. I
don't believe Jesus thought that the devil made Judas betray him. I
don't believe he thought of Satan as anything other than the option
to choose an evil alternative rather than the righteous choice. Satan

64

represents nothing other than the temptation to choose what is not good for you, and prayer is where you struggle with your choices. Whether you imagine that God tests you, or that Satan tempts you, or that you simply have a choice because you are free — prayer is preparation for that moment of choice. I think it is not so strange that Jesus would advise us to:

- Pray, to be not tempted.
- Pray, to make the right choice.
- Pray, to know what to do and do it.

Our prayerful consideration of our options provides guidance, and thereby, deliverance from the consequences of choosing the lesser option. We pray to know God's inner kingdom, not to rule the kingdoms of the world. We pray to align ourselves with God's power and the knowledge to use it wisely. We pray to uplift our consciousness of God, not to be lifted up by God. It took Jesus forty days and nights of prayer and fasting to come to his conclusion. He chose to put these temptations behind him, and commit himself to what he believed was the Truth about himself and the right path for him to take.

Amen!

We pray to realize the Truth, and we are to end our prayer when we are in agreement with Truth. Some say Amen to affirm their agreement with Truth, or with God. Some say Amen to seal the deal. When we know the truth, we are to preserve it, hermetically sealed within us, as a reserve of wisdom and confidence that continues to provide guidance and deliverance. That is what 'Amen' signifies. Remember that the Lord's Prayer is in instruction in how to pray, not what to say. You need not say Amen, but you must reach that point in consciousness where the prayer is complete, and there is nothing more you need to say.

PARABLES OF THE KINGDOM

The kingdom of heaven is like:

- a king, taking account of his servants.

- a king, hosting a wedding reception.

- a man, diversifying his investments.

- a man, hiring laborers for his fields.

- a mustard seed, which a man sowed in his field.

- yeast, which a woman used to make bread.

- a man, who cast seeds into the ground.

- a man, who sowed good seed.

- a net, which a man cast in the sea.

- hidden treasure, which a man finds.

- a merchant man, seeking pearls.

- ten virgins, with oil lamps.

Through parables, Jesus brings heaven down to Earth. No longer beyond reach, God's kingdom is that state in which we live and move and have our being. The kingdom of heaven is a state of being. It is not an event to wait for, or a place to see. It is something to behold, for the kingdom of God is within you, and you within it. The kingdom of heaven is like you and me going about our business, prospering our life.

Parables?

Why didn't Jesus just say what he meant? Here was a man who meant what he said, believed what he said, and intended for others to share in that belief; yet he found it necessary to speak in parables to the crowds and then explain his meaning to the disciples. Parables require interpretation and inner reflection in order to understand the idea being taught. The level of awareness that he hoped to awaken in the listener requires their reflection and leads to intuition and insight. Jesus used parables to provide an opportunity for understanding to occur because there was no opportunity to explain. Tutoring works with a few hand-picked students, but it is not possible with larger crowds of curious listeners. Jesus referred to the crowds as gross, dull and closed-minded. (See Mt. 13:11-15) They were plain and simple folk. The bigger concerns of daily survival filled their minds. They had heard more than enough to dull their senses and were unable to hear his meaning. Jesus gave the answers to his disciples. The rest of us get to ponder the meaning of his words.

Personally, I prefer the parable to the explanation. I would rather be one of the crowd than one of the disciples because I do not like being told what to think. I will tell you what I think, but not what to think. I can tell you what Jesus taught, but not what he thought. The parable provides an opportunity for inspiration, which is more valuable than explanation.

Every analogy is too limited and is eventually replaced by a better analogy, or greater insight. By referring to God as Our Father, Jesus was offering an alternative to thinking of God as king. By teaching parables of the kingdom he was expanding our awareness of the nature of God's realm, beyond the notion of a geopolitical kingdom. Unfortunately for us, that proved to be too much for most people to comprehend.

To this day, religious zealots propagate the idea that their God, or their spiritual leader, is a divine ruler. They promote their religious principles as alternatives to the laws of the lands in which they live. Jesus scrupulously avoided doing that. He said that one should pay their taxes as well as their tithes. (Review Mt. 22:17-22) He said that his kingdom was not of this world. (See Jn. 18:36) He offered an alternative view of the nature of God's kingdom, even so, he was mocked for a claim he did not make (king of the Jews) and crucified for a crime he did not commit: sedition. We owe it to him and ourselves to have a better understanding of what Jesus taught about the nature of God and God's Law.

FORGIVING DEBT
Mt. 18:23-35

Therefore is the kingdom of heaven likened unto a certain king, which would take account of his servants. And when he had begun to reckon, one was brought unto him, which owed him ten thousand talents. But forasmuch as he had not to pay, his lord commanded him to be sold, and his wife, and children, and all that he had, and payment to be made. The servant therefore fell down, and worshipped him, saying, "Lord, have patience with me, and I will pay thee all." Then the lord of that servant was moved with compassion, and loosed him, and forgave him the debt. But the same servant went out, and found one of his fellow servants, which owed him an hundred pence: and he laid hands on him, and took him by the throat, saying, "Pay me that thou owest." And his fellow servant fell down at his feet, and besought him, saying, "Have patience with me, and I will pay thee all." And he would not: but went and cast him into prison, till he should pay the debt. So when his fellow servants saw what was done, they were very sorry, and came and told unto their lord all that was done. Then his lord, after that he had called him, said unto him, "O thou wicked servant, I forgave thee all that debt, because thou desiredst me: Shouldest not thou also have had compassion on thy fellow servant, even as I had pity on thee?" And his lord was wroth, and delivered him to the tormentors, till he should pay all that was due unto him. So likewise shall my heavenly Father do also unto you, if ye from your hearts forgive not every one his brother their trespasses.

Learn Your Lesson

Keep in mind that this parable is an analogy of the state of mind Jesus considered to be heavenly. The story is not to be taken literally. The parables do not provide lessons in social etiquette, family relationships or business practices. The parables are not an instruction manual. In pondering the characters in the story we are supposed to learn the lesson of how to think, not how to behave. We do see examples in life of people behaving just as the characters in the stories, but this is because some people model their behavior and justify their actions on a literal interpretation of Bible stories. Judgment and punishment are not found in Nature, nor are they human nature. They are behaviors we learn by failing to learn the lessons of the parables; and then we teach those behaviors to others. That is the unfortunate aspect of parables: they are often misunderstood. The parables were never intended to be used as a justification for our relations with others, but are instead an interpretation of our relationship with Life, our God.

Lesson Learned

The first lesson to learn in this parable is that your unpaid debts will enslave you. The servant wisely asked for the opportunity to repay all of the debt, so as to avoid defaulting on the loan. The consequences of default would be the loss of his position and separation from his family. The consequences of being at fault are always a sense of loss and separation.

The second lesson is that in life, we get what we ask for. The debtor asked for patience as he repaid all that he owed, and it was extended to him. We also learn that the way one treats others is just another way of asking for it. Because the servant did not have patience with others who owed a debt to him, his own debt was demanded of him.

The lesson to learn is that thoughts determine one's experience of life; not because a higher authority punishes us for what we think, but because we experience the consciousness we express. As we give, it is given unto us. As we do unto others, it is likewise done unto us. Our experience of life can only be for us what Life can become through us.

Consequences

This parable also serves as a warning of the consequences of not being forgiving. As is always the case, the consequences are that it is done unto you as you do unto others. This principle should not be re-written in such a way as to condone retaliation and revenge: Do unto others as they have done unto you. To do so would only show one's ignorance of the compassionate and forgiving nature of our relationship with Life, and it would be a failure to grasp that this principle recommends forgiveness.

If we truly understood the Law of God, we would not try to apply Its principles to our advantage alone. After all, we are not alone in life. We are one with Life. Because our fundamental relationship is with the One, not with one another, we experience in life what we express of Life. To allow what others think, say and do, to be a determining factor in what we think and do is to ignore the nature and principle of our own being. Life can only be for us what It can become through us. Trying to take advantage of others, to retaliate or seek revenge, becomes self-defeating. Regardless of why you would do to others as they have done to you, the principle is still: it is done unto you as you do unto others. Any rationale that seeks to justify mistreatment of others ignores that doing unto others is an act of self-expression, which becomes our experience and affects our consciousness. You can't do harm to another without harming yourself first because what you do is first conceived within you, and then expressed and experienced by you. Every act has a consequence. Even if you think of your act as an unavoidable consequence of their actions, your act has consequences for you. Even if unspoken, your angry word is a poison pill that you must swallow.

Moral of the Story

The moral of this parable may be that if you don't treat others as favorably as Life has treated you, then you will fall out of favor with Life. Why? Well, not because we are judged by God on the basis of how well we treat others. It is because what a infinite and inner God does for us must be done through us. If we are not forgiving, then we aren't expressing forgiveness, and we won't be experiencing forgiveness — for ourselves or anyone else. Even an infinite God can't do for us what It can't do through us. In truth, because It is infinite, It must work from within us, through us, to do anything for us. The infinite cannot work on us, or do anything to us because It is not separate from us. The Infinite One can only do as much for anyone as It can become through that one. So, perhaps the moral is that we are to be (compassionate) and do (forgive) as God is and does.

The Kingdom

My interest in this parable is not so much in its lessons as in what the teachings of Jesus have to say about the kingdom of God. A kingdom defines the realm of the king. It is that the state wherein the presence of the king is revered, and the kings word is respected as Law. The kingdom extends as far as the kings Law is in force. To grasp its fundamental nature we must always keep the location of this kingdom in mind. The heavenly state, according to Jesus, is not the promised land. It is not in the clouds, or in the future. When the Pharisees demanded that he say where and when and how the kingdom of God would come about, he said: "The kingdom of God cometh not with observation: Neither shall they say, Lo here! or, lo there! for, behold, the kingdom of God is within you." (Lk. 17:20-21)

You don't die to get into this heaven; you must live freely. To consciously enter into the kingdom, turn within, and be fully conscious of your relationship with God. The kingdom is that infinite reality in which we live, and move, and have our being. This kingdom is "not of this world"; it is a state of mind. (See Jn. 18:36)

In other parables, this consciousness is represented by a house in which we live, or field in which we sow seeds. A kingdom is that a state where the word, or will, of the King is Law. Parables that use the analogy of kings and kingdoms remind us that we are held accountable by the Law. To be in and of the kingdom of God is to abide by Its Law and to practice Its principles.

The King

A king is the author of the rules or laws that define the kingdom. Therefore, the king is the ruler and authority in the kingdom. The king owns everything, and thus everyone owes their existence to the king. The king is the source and force behind all that happens in the kingdom. At least, these are some of the qualities attributable to a king; qualities that the religious often invest in their God. It was common in Jesus' day to think of God as the king of the universe, the heavens, the hidden spiritual realms. Thinking of God as a king provides a conceptual model for thinking about that which man cannot grasp: an infinite reality. Even the Lord's Prayer, which famously describes God as a Father figure, includes repeated reference to God as king. It is an analogy of reality for which we have no words to describe.

The key to understanding the parables of Jesus is recognition of the main character. Who is represented by the king in this parable? Some consider the king to be God, and I would agree if, and only

73

if, we are thinking of God as an inner presence, the God within us, as us. To think of God in this way, we have to keep in mind the infinite nature of God: It is within and around us, the universal Life individualized as us. If we are thinking of an infinite God, then we can say as Jesus did: "I and *my* Father are one." (Jn. 10:30) We are not one and the same, but one in the sense of inseparable and of the same nature.

Some would rather say that Christ is the King. They prefer to distinguish the inner presence from a universal essence by referring to the presence within as the Christ (the Son), and the universal essence as God (Our Father). The phrase, Christ our Lord, properly refers to the spiritual essence of God within us. It is within us as the Lord (the Law, the governing principle of our being) and as us as the Christ (the individualization of the universal God).

The Christ is what we truly are: a spiritual being. Heaven is our state of mind, our consciousness of being one with God. It is this consciousness, this recognition of one's fundamental nature and being, that allows one to make the audacious claim of being a child of God, the Christ. But, if you truly believe in an infinite God, you must eventually recognize It within you, as you.

So, is God the king or is the Christ the king in our parable? In my opinion, if the kingdom of heaven is my consciousness, then the king of that kingdom must be what I AM. I refer to that infinite Life that is both universal and individualized. I AM is the name of the universal God.

- And Moses said unto God, "Behold, when I come unto the children of Israel, and shall say unto them, The God of your fathers hath sent me unto you; and they shall say to me, What is his name? what shall I say unto them?" And God said unto Moses, "I AM THAT I AM:" and he said, "Thus shalt thou say unto the children of Israel, I AM hath sent me unto you." (Ex. 3:13-14)

74

"I am" is also the way Jesus referred to himself when he was speaking of the Christ, the individualization of God. Many were confused by Jesus' statements, and thought he was speaking blasphemy and nonsense. They thought he referred to his physical nature, but he was speaking of his spiritual nature when he said I am: I am the door, the way, the truth, the light, the vine, the messiah, the Lord, the good shepherd, "… before Abraham was, I am." (Jn.8:58) When Jesus said: "I am not of this world" (Jn. 8:23) he was speaking of himself as the Christ, the individualization of God. (Read all of John 8, for a very interesting conversation of the eternal nature of what we truly are.)

- And Jesus went out, and his disciples, into the towns of Caesarea Philippi: and by the way he asked his disciples, saying unto them, "Whom do men say that I am?" And they answered, "John the Baptist: but some say, Elias; and others, One of the prophets." And he saith unto them, "But whom say ye that I am?" And Peter answereth and saith unto him, "Thou art the Christ." And he charged them that they should tell no man of him. (Mk. 8:27-30)

Why would Jesus' policy be to ask but don't tell, if not because the answer to the question is something each person must recognize for themselves? Of course, some think that the designation of Christ applies only to Jesus, but if we can call God our Father, then we are each a child of God and one with God. We may not all be conscious of the truth of our being, but that does not make it any the less true. Where I am, God is. What I am, God is; and that I AM is the spirit and life that I am. There is one Life. That Life is God. That Life is Perfect. That Life is my life now. At least, that is what I choose to believe about you and me.

The Servant

A literal interpretation of this parable would consider the king to be an ascended spiritual being, a higher power, our Lord, God, Our

Father, etc. The king has servants who are held accountable for how well they serve the Lord. In a literal interpretation, the servants of this supreme being would be all of us human beings who are subject to Its Law.

But, to interpret the story this literally, one would have to think of the kingdom as not quite real and actual, something that is coming, that is yet to be rather than that which we can behold within us now. I have doubts about any interpretation that ignores what the teachings of Jesus clearly state: Behold, the kingdom of God is within you.

If, we think of ourselves as a servant, or consider the various servants to be representative of our many faceted personality, our attitudes and self-concepts, then we have to think of something other than us in the role of king.

Thinking of the king as something other than us, even though we try to locate it within the heavenly kingdom that is our consciousness, instills a sense of separation and duality; which is no more than a literal interpretation of the parable. If we delve no deeper than its literal meaning then we're no longer reading the verses as a parable but as an actual description of the kingdom and our position in it.

Literalists

Those who read the scriptures in this way like to think of themselves as fundamentalists, but they are, more often than not, literalists. A fundamentalist must have some fundamental understanding of the basic concepts. A fundamentalist must be willing to seek a deeper insight than a superficial reading of the written word can provide. True fundamentalism requires a level of thought that is not necessary for a literal interpretation. A literal interpretation relies on definitions. A fundamentalist seeks insight and personal understanding. I am a fundamentalist because I am not satisfied with a literal interpretation of the parables. After all, if the parables were meant to be read literally, then they aren't really parables.

Interpretation

A proper understanding of the parables requires that we realize that they are never about anything other than ourselves. These are stories meant for greater self-awareness. They are not about a distant deity, but the inner spirit. They are not about wealth and riches, but that which has lasting value and virtue. They are not about our relationship with others, but always about our relationship with God. The parables tell the story of one person, and every character in that story is an aspect of this one person: you. The kingdom is your consciousness, and you are the king. The servants are those qualities of consciousness, those thoughts and self-concepts, which serve you.

Accountability

The parable states that the king decided to hold his servants accountable, and found that some concepts serve better than others. Compassion and forgiveness serve better than impatience and judgment. The servants that make a better accounting of themselves are entrusted with more, while others are relegated to lesser roles. Our awareness of the kingdom increases as we realize which thoughts give expression to Life, and which repress it; which principles and practices prosper our life, and which behaviors impoverish it. It is up to us to take an accounting of the concepts that are meant to serve us.

Sad Ending

In my mind, this parable ends on an unfortunate note for the king. At the outset, the king is in a position to forgive, and does so. Later, he is in a position to forgive once again, but does not do so.

It was not a wise decision for it deprived him of the consciousness of forgiveness and left him with a tormented mind.

For the parable to conclude in this manner, the person telling the story must have thought of the king as a wrathful God, and the unforgiving servant as an unfortunate human being. From that point of view, the moral of the story is that if you don't forgive, God won't forgive you. That is one explanation, one point of view, but it is not the way Jesus saw it. It is a literal reading of the verses, and thus does not have the insight one may expect when reading the verses as a parable. When studying the teachings of Jesus we must first determine if we are reading parables or reading instructions that require no further thought on our part.

Agreeable

The king was auditing his books and discovered that one of his servants owed ten thousand talents. A talent is a unit of measure. If it measured gold, this servant owed an astronomical amount. One talent of gold would be worth over a million dollars today, and this servant owed ten thousand times as much. He owed more than he could ever repay. The king was going to sell the servant, his family and possessions as well, to cancel the debt, but instead he forgave the debt. Why? The servant fell down and worshipped him, pleaded for patience and promised to repay all that he owed. The king forgave the debt because he was moved to compassion. He felt what the servant was saying and chose to alleviate his suffering.

A short time later, others servants reported that the servant who was forgiven all his debt had refused to forgive another who owed him a hundred pence, which might amount to a few dollars today. It is difficult to make a financial calculation of the 10,000 talents that were forgiven and the 100 pennies which were not forgiven, but we can say that it amounts to comparing billions to one. Regardless, the point is that the servant who was himself forgiven did not forgive others, which didn't seem fair or just and caused the other servants great sorrow.

Again, the king agreed with this point of view. He turned his attention to the servant he had forgiven, and told him he should have been forgiving. Since he was not of a mind to forgive his fellow servant, the king was no longer of a mind to forgive him. Once again, the king was in agreement with his servants thought on the matter. It seems that all the king does is listen to their counsel and take action as he is moved to by their thought.

This parable describes an interesting aspect of the relationship between the king and the servants: it is an emotional relationship. The king responds by corresponding to the servants, or to put it plainly — we respond to our thoughts. Consider how the king responds to his servants. At first, the king feels and is moved to compassion by his servants passionate pleas. Next, he is judgmental when asked to judge. Then, he condemns those who condemn others. How can one person forgive in one instance and condemn in the next? It is because we can change our mind. It is because we keep our own counsel, and because we have conflicting thoughts on most matters. It is also because it is in our nature to be responsive, to respond by corresponding, and to be in agreement.

Emotional

Our thought has the power to move us, to motivate, to inspire, to require action on our part. What we commonly think of as an emotion is the emotional experience of our thoughts. In response to a thought we are emotional: we sympathize, we feel, we are moved. Our thoughts have the power to stir us up, to move us — up and out of the state of mind we are in, or down to the depths of our awareness.

We name our emotional experience by relating it to the thought that is its cause, in order to better understand and identify it. We say we feel angry when our thought is of anger (angst, pain). We say we feel happy when our thoughts are of happiness (hap, luck, fortune). We say we feel sorrowful, or hopeful, or doubtful when our mind is filled with thoughts of that nature. In naming these feelings, we confer a status they don't really have: existence. Feeling emotion is an experience, not a thing, not an entity, not a spiritual quality, not a devil, not a trait. The ignorant think of emotion as something they possess, or which possess them. Emotion is nothing more (or less) than the experience of thought, but then, that is no small matter in itself. After all, what good is a thought if it can't be experienced, or if it can't move us to a greater awareness? I don't wish to demean emotion, but to understand it for what it is. Emotion is the experience of a thinker, alone with his thought.

Forgive and Forget

It now seems that the moral of the story is to forgive and forget. The servant may have forgotten how much he owed to the king, but the king did not forget. The servant was called to account, and since he had nothing with which to pay the debt, the debt was forgiven. Why should the king forgive what could not be repaid? Why not? If he forgives, then he can forget about it.

The servant was relieved of his debt; but obviously did not believe in forgiveness, as he would not forgive a debt owed to him. Even though he had been forgiven, he didn't forgive or forget debts, and consequently, he could no longer forget his debt, and was tormented by the thought of it forever. If you are forgiven, never forget it. If you can't forgive, forget about being forgiven.

But lest we get caught up in the parable, let us remember that while this is a story with many characters, it is about only one person: the person who is in a position to forgive. It is about the consciousness of forgiveness. The person who forgives expresses and experiences forgiveness. The person who will not forgive, forsakes forgiveness. And while forgiveness can be requested of others, or of God, forgiveness can only be experienced by those who forgive. Jesus stated that the Father judges no man, for all judgment has been given to the Son (you and I included). We have the ability to judge, but it is not advisable. He taught: "Judge not, and ye shall not be judged: condemn not, and ye shall not be condemned: forgive, and ye shall be forgiven." (Lk. 6:37)

Why? We are forgiven, not because God is moved with compassion by our compassionate act, but because we are moved by the thought of forgiveness, by our desire for it and the opportunity to express it. We are forgiven because the forgiveness we express is the forgiveness we experience. We know forgiveness at the moment and to the extent that we forgive.

THE WEDDING RECEPTION
Mt. 22:2-14

The kingdom of heaven is like unto a certain king, which made a marriage for his son, And sent forth his servants to call them that were bidden to the wedding: and they would not come. Again, he sent forth other servants, saying, "Tell them which are bidden, Behold, I have prepared my dinner: my oxen and my fatlings are killed, and all things are ready: come unto the marriage." But they made light of it, and went their ways, one to his farm, another to his merchandise: And the remnant took his servants, and entreated them spitefully, and slew them. But when the king heard thereof, he was wroth: and he sent forth his armies, and destroyed those murderers, and burned up their city. Then saith he to his servants, "The wedding is ready, but they which were bidden were not worthy. Go ye therefore into the highways, and as many as ye shall find, bid to the marriage." So those servants went out into the highways, and gathered together all as many as they found, both bad and good: and the wedding was furnished with guests. And when the king came in to see the guests, he saw there a man which had not on a wedding garment: And he saith unto him, "Friend, how camest thou in hither not having a wedding garment?" And he was speechless. Then said the king to the servants, "Bind him hand and foot, and take him away, and cast him into outer darkness; there shall be weeping and gnashing of teeth." For many are called, but few are chosen.

R.S.V.P.

Jesus told the story of the wedding as a parable of the celebration of Life, the heavenly state of marriage, where two become as one. The invitations went out, and the RSVPs did not come back. Why not? The guests were called, and still they would not come. They were too busy. Too busy to celebrate? Too busy to accept a feast? Too busy to enjoy life? It seems so: "... they made light of it, and went their ways, one to his farm, another to his merchandise" (Mt. 22:3-5) If you think there is no reason to celebrate this day, or that there will always be another opportunity, then you will always be too busy. And one day you'll be too late.

The problem is not that we have important work to do, work that won't wait and responsibilities that can't be ignored. The problem is that we make light of the opportunity that this day holds. We demean the day, thinking there will always be another day. And there will, but the fact that there will be a good reason to celebrate each day does not make this day any the less significant. How ironic that our belief in endless opportunity justifies rejecting the opportunity at hand. Believing in the future good, we ignore the good that is given!

It is understandable that we give priority to our work; for the principle is first sow, and then reap. If you do not sow, you will have nothing to reap; but, if you do not reap, you will have nothing to sow! What are you working for, if not to enjoy the fruits of your labor? Are you working so that others might enjoy? How altruistic; but that is not the principle Jesus taught. His idea was that we should do unto others as we would have them do unto us; which presumes that you will accept the good they do for you. There is no sense in doing good for others and not accepting the good they offer you. It is as unreasonable as making time to sow a field, but not taking time to reap the harvest. Replace your belief in a future reward with acceptance of that good now. Please, respond in the affirmative to Life's invitation to a celebration.

Ambivalence

Some respond to invitations and opportunities with ambivalence: "I don't care." Ambivalence sounds similar to equivalence, and we may think that it expresses a well-balanced state of non-attachment to either option, but it doesn't. The ambivalent do not wish to choose, professing no strong desire for one or the other, but if you press for an RSVP, a decision, you may find a level of emotion behind their refusal that belies the well-balanced facade: "I DON'T CARE!" It is not that they don't wish to choose. They are unable to choose because of strong conflicting emotions. We may wish to accept, but we reject. We may wish to love, but find ourselves angry with those whom we love. Ambivalence is not a balanced emotional state. It is a state of inner conflict, with an initial calm that is a prelude to a storm. Imagine the shock for the servants who were calling on the guests, merely asking for a yes or no, when treated with spite: malice and murder. "And the remnant took his servants, and entreated them spitefully, and slew them." (Mt. 22:6)

"I don't care," is a statement of repressed love. It is the refusal to love. It is the rejection of that which you would love to accept. It is the negation of the positive. The reality is that we do care; we do have a preference. Our nature is loving and accepting. We care, but our judgments stand in the way of a decision. We judge the facts and appearances so that we might make the right, the good, the true, the lovely choice. How ironic then that our judgments make it difficult, if not impossible, to express our love. Love: judge naught.

Propriety

In Jesus's wedding story, as in life, a man was invited who would have accepted a seat at the table, but he was ill-prepared to enjoy the celebration. He did not dress appropriately for the occasion. "Friend, how camest thou in hither not having a wedding garment?" Certainly, we've all seen this happen with family and friends who show up for dinner, looking worn and tattered. But, have you ever noticed that those who insist: "Take me as I am" are usually at their worst at that moment? It is as if they present themselves as a challenge to our ability to overlook their appearance or behavior, a challenge to love and accept them.

And certainly, we have all turned down invitations because we weren't dressed for it, or couldn't be ready in time. We'd rather not go than go and feel out of place, and out of place is what we'd be if we went to a party without dressing for the party. The party dress is part of the celebration. It is part of what makes for the celebration. If you show up in work clothes or casual dress, you are obviously there to eat and drink, but add nothing to the celebration. You are out of place and will have to leave, or be thrown out.

- "Bind him hand and foot, and take him away, and cast him into outer darkness; there shall be weeping and gnashing of teeth."

For many are called, but few are chosen. (Mt. 22:14)

Many answer the call, but few make the choices necessary to enjoy the celebration of life. I'd like to feel sorry for the man who was tossed out of the wedding reception, to think the host treated him rudely and unfairly. After all, he wasn't there testing the patience of his host. He didn't have a smart answer for why he was not well dressed for the occasion, but ignorance provides no excuse in life. Being ignorant of the Law doesn't excuse you from its consequences. "I didn't know," won't make it all right.

The choices they make, and the choices they don't make, keep them from entering into the celebration of Life. Why are so few acceptable? It is because so few accept the opportunity and choose

85

appropriately. It was an equal opportunity occasion, but that only means that anyone may apply. Everyone may enter in, but only those who can meet the requirements can fulfill them, finding fulfillment in the opportunity.

The party was open to all, but that didn't make it a "free for all." An open invitation doesn't lessen the standards or requirements of a holy celebration. When Moses communed with God, the first thing he was told was: "... put off thy shoes from off thy feet, for the place whereon thou standest is holy ground." (Ex. 3:5) Even at a realtor's open house, everyone is still expected to remove their shoes at the door. All may enter into Life, but the Laws of Life still apply. We must be appropriately attired, having the proper character and disposition, worthy of the consciousness of the celebration.

Opportunity

Some men may find in this parable a ready excuse for not attending wedding receptions. "I've got nothing to wear, and after all, look what happened to that poor fellow in the Bible." When we do not think or feel equal to the opportunity, we tend to refuse it. That would be a mistake. The thing to do is dress yourself appropriately, which begins with addressing yourself appropriately. "I am not equal," is a denial of yourself. It is a statement of fact, not an expression of truth, and it is a negative statement at that. It negates the truth of your being: I am equal to every opportunity that confronts me. I wouldn't recognize the opportunity as such if I didn't have it within me to fulfill it. I wouldn't be standing at the door if I had not received an invitation. Someone must think I'm equal, and I pray that I am that one.

Some may think they are equal, even more than equal, but not quite ready yet. "I am not ready," is equivalent to "I am not equal." It is a compromise, and an attempt at avoidance. It is praying for the opportunity to pass by you. It reminds me of the

86

clergywoman who travelled to India to attend an audience with the Dali Lama. She missed the appointment because it took her too long to decide what to wear to it. Perhaps your opportunity will still be there when you are ready to accept it.

What we must accept is that we are equal to the opportunity, and that takes faith. Opportunity is a favorable wind that fills your sails and brings you to port. It is the power of Life to get you where you are headed. However, Life only does for you what It can do through you, and if you are not ready, if you think you are not ready, if you don't feel ready, then Life can do nothing with you or for you. Nevertheless, you truly are ready for what Life offers. The opportunity is yours to accept, or not.

TALENTS
Mt. 25:14-30

For the kingdom of heaven is as a man traveling into a far country, who called his own servants, and delivered unto them his goods. And unto one he gave five talents, to another two, and to another one; to every man according to his several ability; and straightway took his journey. Then he that had received the five talents went and traded with the same, and made them other five talents. And likewise he that had received two, he also gained other two. But he that had received one went and digged in the earth, and hid his lord's money. After a long time the lord of those servants cometh, and reckoneth with them. And so he that had received five talents came and brought other five talents, saying, "Lord, thou deliveredst unto me five talents: behold, I have gained beside them five talents more." His lord said unto him, "Well done, thou good and faithful servant: thou hast been faithful over a few things, I will make thee ruler over many things: enter thou into the joy of thy lord." He also that had received two talents came and said, "Lord, thou deliveredst unto me two talents: behold, I have gained two other talents beside them." His lord said unto him, "Well done, good and faithful servant; thou hast been faithful over a few things, I will make thee ruler over many things: enter thou into the joy of thy lord." Then he which had received the one talent came and said, "Lord, I knew thee that thou art an hard man, reaping where thou hast not sown, and gathering where thou hast not strawed: And I was afraid, and went and hid thy talent in the earth: lo, there thou hast that is thine." His lord answered and said unto him, "Thou wicked and slothful servant, thou knewest that I reap where I sowed not, and gather where I have not strawed: Thou oughtest therefore to have put my money to the exchangers, and then at my coming I should have received mine own with usury. Take therefore the talent from him, and give it unto him which hath ten talents. For unto every one that hath shall be given, and he shall have abundance: but from him that hath not shall be taken away even that which he hath. And cast ye the unprofitable servant into outer darkness: there shall be weeping and gnashing of teeth."

Kingdom of Heaven

The kingdom of heaven is one's consciousness. It is where we turn to commune with God. It is a realm of divine Law, where God's principles prosper those who keep them. The kingdom is the household wherein the head of the house and the servants work to the benefit of all. In this parable, we are given an insight as to how the kingdom of heaven works when the head of the house is not present. This man who journeys to a far country is referred to as the lord of his servants. His role in the parable is to represent you, the thinker, the one whose word is law, or rather it is supposed to be in his own house and with his own servants.

Lord

Do not let the fact that the man is referred to as the lord of his servants confuse you as to whom he represents. He does not represent the Christ, even though Jesus was called lord by the disciples who served him. The term 'lord' defines the man's role in his household: he is to keep the Law in mind, while directing his servants, who serve him. Whoever has the role of head of the house has the responsibility of managing the affairs of that house in a lawful manner, in a prosperous manner, in a wholesome manner which benefits all.

When we read that the lord was: "hard man, reaping where thou hast not sown, and gathering where thou hast not strawed:" This means that he expected to profit from the work of his servants. He expected his thought and intelligence, his talents and abilities, to make more money for him than he could make through his own labor. He considered the proper use of wealth to be profitability, increase, more abundance. But before reviewing those dynamics, let me remind you of what the other elements of the parable represent.

Far Country

The "far country" represents a sense of separation from the source of one's well-being, a state of mind that Jesus also described in the Parable of the Prodigal Son. The prodigal left his father's house with all his goods, journeying to a far country, where there was riotous living followed by famine and degradation. In this state of mind, he wasted all he had. However, in the Parable of the Talents, before the man journeyed to a far country, he invested his wealth with his servants.

Servants

Remember, these are servants in a mental household. The servants represent the conscious thoughts, beliefs, attitudes and self-concepts which are supposed to serve the will of the head of the house. They reside in consciousness. It is our consciousness that he refers to as the kingdom of heaven. The servants serve within you. You are not one of the servants in this kingdom. You are the head of the house. There is no one above you, doing your thinking for you, taking on your responsibilities and telling you what to do. Your will directs and organizes your thought in a way that works for you. How well it works is not a matter of your good intentions but of how effective and worthwhile your thoughts are. Two of the servants were called good and faithful, for they had prospered the household by using and increasing what had been entrusted to their care. One of the servants proved to be unprofitable and was called wicked and slothful.

Talents

The varying amounts of talents entrusted to the servants point out the obvious: some start with more than others. We may wonder why this is so, and think that having more to start with is advantageous, but the story doesn't support this idea. Each servant is rewarded according to the percentage of their increase, not the amount. They are rewarded for what they do with what they have.

And why at the outset are some entrusted with more than others? In life, it is given "to every man according to his several ability;" Our abilities are what we start with; which is why we have come to refer to them as talents. Of course, some of us have talents that others do not have. In some aspects of life, one will have a greater capacity than another due to the circumstances that make us all unique individuals. The infinite Life is the source of us all and yet some are short and others tall; some are large and others small. An acorn and an apple seed planted side by side will draw from nature all they can in order to become what they must be. Who would wish to say that one has an advantage over the other, or that one is preferable to the other? Perhaps the envious, the jealous, the foolish who do not fully appreciate themselves, but not I. According to this parable, the only distinction is between those who invest their talents, and those who bury them. It makes no difference how many talents you have to start with, if none are being used then it is as if you had none. If you use only one, it is as if you had only one. Increase and prosperity are not a matter of our potential, but the actual investment we make in life. How much we will eventually have to work with, is a matter of putting what we had to start with, to good use. It is not favoritism or random chance, but the impartial nature of how it works that determines what each person will have to use.

In nature, we see that a shallow creek carries only a little water, but over time the creek deepens into a stream and then a river. As it can then allow for greater flow, it receives a greater quantity. The water flowing through it makes for a deeper channel, but the amount of water it has carried is not why the river gets more than a stream. It gets more because it is deeper and, therefore, able to carry more.

My point, and I think the point of this parable, is that we should not think we would have been more profitable if only we had received more to begin with; nor should we think that having a comparatively small amount to work with provides us with an excuse. We receive according to our ability to use, and we get more as we prove that we can use more.

The talents in this parable are often considered to be qualities endowed by God, natural abilities that are unique to that individual. We call these inherent abilities talents because of this parable.The talents in this parable refer to the amount of gold or silver each received. A talent was a unit of measure. Even one talent would be the equivalent of over a million dollars today. The servant who received the one talent was not being slighted. The servant who received five talents was not being favored. Each was being entrusted with an investment. Each servant received (according to their unique abilities) a great wealth with the anticipation that it would increase, for that is what it means to be of service. It makes no difference if we are talking about an investment of gold, or God-given talents, or seed corn. We should expect whatever we have of value to increase by the proper use of it. And if it doesn't, someone is going to be held accountable for the lost opportunity.

A Reckoning

The parable states that eventually there was an inevitable accounting, a reckoning. Some people think of being held accountable as Judgment Day, where God judges the worth of their souls. To interpret the parable in this way, you have to consider yourself to be one of the servants, and the lord to be the Christ or God. I've already stated my objection to this point of view, but there is one other reason to not accept such an interpretation: it requires that Jesus or God judge others. Again, if you think of yourself as a servant, you either hope to be judged or fear that judgment (according to how you have judged yourself). But this belief in being judged contradicts the teachings of Jesus on judgment.

- "For the Father judgeth no man, but hath committed all judgment unto the Son:" (Jn. 5:22)
- And one of the company said unto him, "Master, speak to my brother, that he divide the inheritance with me." And he said unto him, "Man, who made me a judge or a divider over you?" (Lk. 12:13-14)
- "Judge not, that ye be not judged." (Mt. 7:1)

It seems that since Jesus spoke against divisive judgment that he would be hypocritical to judge others, and we would be foolish to think that he would or should. All judgment is self-judgment. Whether we are conscious of judging ourselves or think we are judging others, the consequence is the same: our judgment judges us.

- "For with what judgment ye judge, ye shall be judged: and with what measure ye mete, it shall be measured to you again." (Mt. 7:2)

Though no one can pass sentence on another, everyone is held accountable in life, by Life. To think otherwise is to think, wish, or hope that your thought and actions are inconsequential. There are always consequences. Though it may take a long time to realize, it was always there working its way to the surface like the fruit hidden in the seed. The only reason to fear the consequences, the reckoning, is that you know the quality of your thought and action.

In this parable, it is not people, but ideas that are being held accountable for their quality, their profitability. The question being asked is: does it work or not? Those which proved their profitability, their ability to handle a little bit in a prosperous manner, received work. Let's remember: the profit was the lords, and the servant only got the opportunity to work on bigger projects. The head of the house prospers as the household prospers; and this is due to profitable servants. The head of the house had checked out, leaving his faithful servants to work for him. Some proved more faithful than others.

The servant who received one talent was fearful, not faithful. Afraid that he was not equal to the task, and fearing the consequences of failure, he failed: he didn't try. He buried his talent. His reasoning was that he could avoid loss by not trying to be profitable. He could avoid loss by not using the only valuable thing that had been entrusted to him. This servant represents the idea that the avoidance of loss is profitability, and preferable to using and risking what you have. But, attempting to avoid loss leads to the experience of loss (regret: weeping, wailing, gnashing teeth) and then to actual loss (rejected: outer darkness). If we can't make our way in the world, we'll lose our way in the world. If we don't or won't use it, we lose it. That is a natural occurrence in life. We might even consider it a principle of Life.

The Haves

It is better to be a 'have' than a 'have-not,' but let's realize what the "haves" have that the "have-nots" do not. It is not money. It is knowledge of what works in life. They have faith, and that is nothing more or less than the expectation that the application of the principle will work in a way that prospers. Fear is nothing other than a lack of faith. The servant who lost all had already lost all his faith. Losing what little he was still managing to hold onto was inevitable. The loss of faith is terminal because it leaves one with the belief that nothing works, nothing will work, so why bother to work? Such an idea cannot hope to be gainfully employed.

For unto every one that hath [faith] shall be given, and he shall have abundance: but from him that hath not [faith] shall be taken away even that which he hath. The issue isn't fear, but faith or the lack thereof. Some people report that they still have fears even as they apply their faith to the task at hand, and they report that it works. They also say that there are still shadows after you light a candle, but you have light by which to make your way. We needn't struggle with our fears. In fact, this parable suggests that we simply fire them! Eject them from our conscious consideration and entrust all our attention and resources to those concepts and attitudes that work!

A PENNY A DAY
Mt. 20:1-16

For the kingdom of heaven is like unto a man that is an householder, which went out early in the morning to hire labourers into his vineyard. And when he had agreed with the labourers for a penny a day, he sent them into his vineyard. And he went out about the third hour, and saw others standing idle in the marketplace, And said unto them; "Go ye also into the vineyard, and whatsoever is right I will give you." And they went their way. Again he went out about the sixth and ninth hour, and did likewise. And about the eleventh hour he went out, and found others standing idle, and saith unto them, "Why stand ye here all the day idle?" They say unto him, "Because no man hath hired us." He saith unto them, "Go ye also into the vineyard; and whatsoever is right, that shall ye receive." So when even was come, the lord of the vineyard saith unto his steward, "Call the labourers, and give them their hire, beginning from the last unto the first." And when they came that were hired about the eleventh hour, they received every man a penny. But when the first came, they supposed that they should have received more; and they likewise received every man a penny. And when they had received it, they murmured against the goodman of the house, Saying, "These last have wrought but one hour, and thou hast made them equal unto us, which have borne the burden and heat of the day." But he answered one of them, and said, "Friend, I do thee no wrong: didst not thou agree with me for a penny? Take that thine is, and go thy way: I will give unto this last, even as unto thee. Is it not lawful for me to do what I will with mine own? Is thine eye evil, because I am good?" So the last shall be first, and the first last: for many be called, but few chosen.

The Principle

Give some thought to the role that money plays in a parable. There were no pennies in ancient times. The coin in this parable was a denarius. It had approximately a tenth of an ounce of gold or silver content. In other parables, we read of talents of gold. The talent is not a coin. It is a unit of weight, representing approximately seventy pounds of gold or silver. In some parables, we are confronted with a wealth so great that its value in gold is measured in pounds, and in other parables only a minuscule amount is involved. We read of servants who are entrusted with one, two, and five talents, and we read of another servant who owed ten thousand talents! And in this parable, people are quibbling over a penny? If we factor inflation, and the variables of currency exchange rates, that penny might be worth a few dollars today while a talent would be the equivalent of millions of dollars. You can do the math, but the practical distinction is that a denarius is a coin you can hold in your hand while a talent is much more than you can hold. When we read of a wage of a penny a day, the issue at hand is not an hourly rate. The penny is irrelevant. It is the principle that matters. The monetary value is not relevant to the parable. Whether we are asked to consider pennies or talents is irrelevant. Both represent amounts that are either too small or too large to be an issue. It is the principle that matters.

The Workhouse

Jesus likens heaven to the experience of being a householder, one who has a household and the responsibilities that go with it:

the head of the house. That doesn't sound heavenly, but I guess it depends on who you ask. A servant in that household may think so, but if you ask the head of the house, the answer may be no. But perhaps this is due to the way we think of heaven, rather than any detrimental aspects of having a household to manage. We tend to think of heaven as a blissful state where one is taken care of, rather than that state wherein everyone, and everything, works! Wouldn't that be wonderful? If you liked your work, then that would be heavenly.

In the parables, the householder owns his own house. He is so to speak the lord of his castle, in charge of his servants and responsible for his estate, his fields, his vineyard, etc. In more recent times, this house might be described as a cottage industry. It was the place wherein you dwelled, worked, played, prayed and lived out your life. At certain times of the year, there was more work than the household could accomplish without hired help. The householder hired day laborers at the going rate: a penny for a twelve hour day. But as the day, and the work progressed, there was a need for more laborers in the field; so the householder continued to hire help throughout the day. The laborers hired at the beginning of the day agreed to a penny. The laborers hired throughout the day were promised "whatsoever is right."

At the end of the day, some had labored all day, and some for as little as one hour, but all received the same pay! Was that right? Those who had bargained for a penny did not think it was right that those who labored only a few hours should receive the same compensation as those who labored all day. But the householder vigorously defended his actions as his right, and the right thing for him to do.

It is understandable that those who were on the job first felt they deserved a greater compensation than those who were the last to report for work. However, understanding their complaint is not the lesson of this parable. Understanding why the householder considered equal pay just compensation would be more insightful.

Equity

We like to assert that no one is greater than another, and this leads us to affirm that no one is less than another. If we think that there is no greater or lesser among us, then we must think we are equals; however, to think this way requires a universal perspective. I think Ralph Waldo Emerson said it best: "There is no great and no small to the Soul that maketh all." From God's point of view, we are all equals. From an infinite perspective, all is one. We are all perceived to be one with God, each an individualization of the One Life, and, therefore, equal in nature and essence, but is that the way we see it? Do we not think of some others as less than ourselves, and some as greater? What is it that makes us think we are equal, one with another? Is it an equal start, or an equal finish? Is it an equal opportunity or an equal achievement? Is it that we treat one another as equals, or that we are treated by Life Itself as equals?

The parable provides a clue in its summation. The last shall be first, and the first shall be last. The last to enter the field shall receive as much as the first, and the first to enter the field shall receive as much as the last. In that, they are equal.

Remember: they all received the same amount. The last did not get more (or less), and the first did not get less (or more). We are so used to the notion that being first in line is better than being last in line that we assume there is (or should be) some greater benefit for those who are first in line, or first to cross the line. But in this parable all received an equal amount. That is just, but only if you receive it just because you show up for work. It may be just if it is only a signing bonus: an equal amount for all who sign on to work. But, if so, then what is the compensation for working in the field? And, how can an equal amount be equitable, considering that some have worked longer than others?

Compensation

One possible answer is that the compensation for working in the field is that you get to work in the field! Your work is your compensation. The reward of doing a good deed is in doing it; isn't it? If you are doing the work you love, what more could you ask?

Survey the employees of any business as to who is receiving the greater compensation: those who arrive early and stay late, or those who arrive late and take off early? Those who think they deserve more for putting in longer hours at work might also expect to have more fun and enjoyment than anyone else by being the first to arrive and the last to leave the party. But, ask the host and hostess that catered the party, whether or not they had the most fun. Or, consider why it is traditional for the bride and groom to leave their party before the guests leave. They arrive last and leave first because we wish them to have the most fun! A late arrival and early departure seem to work as well as, or better than, staying all day. But now I am just restating the situation described in the parable.

Still, it doesn't seem fair for everyone to receive the same compensation for unequal time and effort. The fact that this occurs is not in question. The question is why it is so; and why doesn't it seem fair to us? Why do we expect to have a greater compensation for being the first to arrive at the party, or for staying at a picnic all day, or being awake to see the sunrise and then enjoy the sunset? Will those who waited hours to see the sun set be treated to more beauty than those who lifted their gaze just in time? What can we expect to get for entering into Life? A life! We get to work, and play and pray and live out our life. Fulfillment does not occur at the end of the day, but throughout the day, when you are doing your work, the work you love.

Those who work longer get to do more work, and thus achieve more than those who only get to work for an hour or two. They experience greater achievement, greater accomplishment, greater enjoyment and fulfillment. Don't they? They do if they love their work. But even so, the greater good they receive or perceive is not compensation. Compensation is payment for loss: loss of time and energy; lost opportunity. We expect compensation for work we don't enjoy, work we would rather not do, work that does not profit us. Working in the 'Lord's vineyard' must be considered a privilege, a blessing. That work is its own reward. If that is the case, then those who enter in late will have the same experience as those who came earlier. The early birds cannot complain for they've enjoyed working in the fields longer than those who came in the last hour. They have received more as they have invested more of themselves in their labors. Instead of complaining, they might exclaim to the newcomer: Better late than never.

You

If not you, then who? Who is the lord in this parable? For that matter, who are the laborers, and the steward? Who is the householder supposed to be? To understand the parables we must remember that this is a story about one person (you), and everything that plays a significant role in the story is some aspect of that one person.

You are a householder. In this parable, you own a field as well: you are the lord of the vineyard. In Jesus' parables, the house represents one's consciousness, and the field (vineyard) represents the creative nature of one's consciousness. Your thought becomes your experience, in consciousness and the circumstances that result from that consciousness.

You also have a steward, and probably other servants, as well as the day-laborers you've hired. They represent concepts and qualities of consciousness that serve you: beliefs, attitudes, ideas, choices, etc. Some serve you better than others. The laborers hired from the first hour to the last represent the tried and true, augmented by trying something new.

Fulfillment

Notice that the new does not replace the old, but augments it and fulfills the work that is at hand. Hiring more and more laborers throughout the day indicates a willingness on the part of the householder to do what works. Remember that the parable tells the story of what it is like for one to enter into the consciousness of heaven, and Jesus' ministry was dedicated to fulfilling the prophecies of God's kingdom. He said: "Think not that I am come to destroy the law, or the prophets: I am not come to destroy, but to fulfill." (Mt. 5:17)

That is the attitude Jesus took, and the attitude the householder took toward getting the work done. As long as there is work to do, keep trying new ideas to get it done. Jesus promoted a new concept of heaven, and a novel approach to fulfilling old prophecies. If the old ways have not done the job, why not try something new? Why not? It is usually because we are not trying to get the work done; we are trying to prove a point. But if we can't prove it, then it is time to change our mind and change our ways. If those who have labored long still have more than they can do, then bring in the new. Jesus advised: "The harvest truly *is* plenteous, but the labourers *are few*; Pray ye therefore the Lord of the harvest, that he will send forth labourers into his harvest." (Mt. 9:37-38) The kingdom of heaven is as a person who uses the old and the new, the tried and the true, all the assets and talents available to him. We will have to be more accepting to get the work done.

Literal / Parable

Most people read the Bible searching for information on God, and how to relate to God. They read these parables to discern which character portrays God, and which role in the story tells their own story. However, we must remember that parables were told in such way that the hearer must search within for insights and understanding of their relationship with God. A literal reading misses the point. A literal reading of a parable may seem to offer advice on relationships with others. but it provides no personal, spiritual, insight. A superficial reading of the parable may find a role for God by finding a subservient role for oneself. One could assign the role of lord of the vineyard to God, and assign to oneself multiple roles: householder, steward, and laborers. As I've stated, we tend to look for God in parables, but this is not a parable about God, but of the kingdom of God. It is a parable that describes the inner kingdom of heaven as the consciousness of a man that is a householder. It is a parable about every one of us. It provides insights into our nature, not the nature of God.

Aside from this reason for not downgrading the main character from householder to steward, there is the first sentence of the parable to contend with: "For the kingdom of heaven is like unto a man that is an householder, which went out early in the morning to hire labourers into his vineyard." (Mt. 20:1) The central figure in this story is you! You are a householder. You are the lord of your vineyard. You set the rate, determine the worth, and get the work done. I point this out because there is a strong tendency to read the parables for the moral of the story, not the meaning. The moral of the story might be that the last shall be first, and the first shall be last; which is encouraging to those who think, "better late than never," is true. Or perhaps it is better to not try to strike a bargain with Life, and just accept whatever is right. Whatever the moral, a possible meaning is clear to me: It will take a steady infusion of new thoughts to find fulfillment in what you've been working on for so long.

Lord's Work

But again, my point of view is predicated on the idea that doing the work of the Lord provides its own reward. What kind of work might that be? Being loving and caring might be an example of being fully employed in a way for which there is no adequate compensation, other than the opportunity to be loving. Would it make any sense to say to a loved one: "Look at how long I've loved and cared for you. Am I not entitled to more appreciation and a greater compensation than others?" *(Well, you've gotten all you're going to get out of that relationship!)* If you wish to claim that you sacrificed and suffered losses, then you can ask for compensation, but you can't gripe about what you get while doing what you love to do, what you agreed to do, especially when it profits you.

In that circumstance, it would be shameful to ask for further compensation, or to think others should get less than you because of your seniority. It would be like a grandparent complaining that their grandchild was enjoying life far too much for someone so young. Ridiculous! Those who are new to life have a right to as much as their elders, who in most cases have bargained for less. When one enters into Life, they get the whole of life, all at once, and they then embrace, embody and accept all that they can. They are not being compensated, nor will they be. They get what is right for them, because they get what they can accept of all that God provides.

A Given

A "given" is what Life has to offer. What It has to offer has already been given! Whatever is right, whatever is just, whatever can be given equally to all is what Life offers. You have to work for the rest. Remember what Jesus considered to be the model of righteous giving: "… he maketh his sun to rise on the evil and on the good, and sendeth rain on the just and on the unjust." (Mt. 5:45) In reviewing Mt. 5:43-48, we find that we are to do as God does so that we might be perfect even as God is. We are to be loving and generous, not only to those who love and give to us, but to everyone, equally. We are to be respectful and helpful, even to

104

those whom we would judge to be undeserving. Why? Why not? What reward is there in trading compliments and gifts? Do something good for someone, in a way they cannot compensate you, and your reward is in heaven (within you). You'll know the good you've done, and that you are at heart, good; and you can't put a price on the value that has for your life and well-being.

A MUSTARD SEED
Mt. 13:31-32

The kingdom of heaven is like to a grain of mustard seed,
which a man took, and sowed in his field: Which indeed is the
least of all seeds: but when it is grown, it is the greatest among
herbs, and becometh a tree, so that the birds of the air come
and lodge in the branches thereof.

Creative Process
How can the kingdom be like a mustard seed? It can't. That is
one of the points that Jesus was making: our concept of the
presence of God is too limited. We should get beyond the idea of
the kingdom and think in terms of the creative process, such as
planting a seed in the soil. Whether sowing a seed in our field or
instilling a concept in the mental field of our soul, we are working
with God's Law.

Having a concept of God is like planting the mustard seed,
which starts out small, yet grows as big as a tree. The
consciousness of God is an idea that grows and evolves over time
into a greater awareness. Our knowledge of the nature of God is
infinitesimal, but this fundamental idea of the inner presence of
Life has the potential to inspire great understanding.

Faith
Jesus associated the mustard seed with the idea of faith, for that
too is a concept that evolves into greater knowledge. We can
understand faith as our consciousness of the presence of God at
work within and through us. Like the seed becomes a tree, our faith
in the presence of God not only becomes greater over time, it also
provides support for other spiritual qualities and concepts, like the
branches of a tree provide a roost for the birds.

The growth of a seed is as much a process of Law as the actions of the King in his Kingdom, and that is the value of this simple parable. It provides an alternative to the analogy of a kingdom. Our concept of the presence of God in our lives does not need to echo what we've heard about for centuries. Our concept of heaven can be as simple as birds singing in the trees, or manna provided for our daily bread. (See Ex. 16:13-15)

LEAVEN
Mt. 13:33

The kingdom of heaven is like unto leaven, which a woman took, and hid in three measures of meal, till the whole was leavened.

Yeast

Leaven is the yeast that supplies the chemical process by which dough rises to become 'risen' bread. In this parable, a little bit of yeast, hidden within a lot of meal, can raise the whole amount. As such, it represents a transformative process: a spiritual awareness or consciousness that uplifts us — heart, soul, and mind. The parable of the leaven is similar to the parable of the mustard seed, wherein the least of seeds can become the greatest of herbs.

Measure

But there is more to consider, in the description of the meal. It is a whole made up of three measures. The yeast doesn't work on only part of the whole. It keeps working until the whole rises, which is impressive given the amounts involved. Three measures are approximately 60 pounds of meal. That would make one huge loaf of bread! In Jesus' parables, the amounts were always very large; not to impress us with the size but to point out that the amount didn't matter with respect to the principle involved. Given time, the yeast grows and increases as required to accomplish the task of wholeness.

The leaven is a thought hidden in one's consciousness. One achieves a sense of wholeness when each measure of consciousness has risen. What is the measure of a man? What is the measure by which we evaluate one's consciousness? Jesus answered that question: "Thou shalt love the Lord thy God with all thy heart, and with all thy soul, and with all thy mind." (Mt. 22:37)

We have not fulfilled the commandment until we have fulfilled all three measures of it. We do not wholly love until we have a loving heart, loving soul, and loving mind.

Heaven

The kingdom of heaven is that state of consciousness wherein we are wholly loving. Many people are conflicted, having achieved only one measure of love. Many people profess a love of God, but they don't forgive or forget. Many people love someone, but not themselves, or anyone else. There are times when we'd love to love, but our soul is in pain and our mind is too confused to know what to say or do. But to be conscious of the kingdom of heaven is to know the perfect love that uplifts us — heart, soul and mind — until we are wholly inspired.

In this parable, love is the leaven, and heaven is that state of being wholly inspired by love. But in other verses, Jesus uses leaven to refer to the teachings and the consciousness of the Pharisees. He tells the disciples that they must have a greater 'leaven' than the Pharisees and that they should beware of the leaven / hypocrisy of the Pharisees. The Pharisees appeared to be righteous, holy men, but Jesus condemned them for leading the people astray and standing in the way of those who seek to enter the kingdom of heaven. The leaven of the Pharisees is not going to raise, uplift or transform the individual; whereas Jesus considered his parables of the kingdom to be transformative.

Unleavened Bread

It is not necessary to draw out the analogy any further, but I find it interesting that unleavened bread is used to commemorate the Passover and escape from Egypt. It is the bread made in haste. It is the bread associated with the Israelites time of wandering in the desert. Only when they have their own land, their own kingdom, only then are they instructed to bake leavened bread as an offering to God. It may be reading too much into the parable, but one could argue that the leaven of the Pharisees kept the people wandering and wondering when the kingdom would return. The leaven of Jesus' teachings inspired them to turn within, and behold the kingdom of God. (See Lk. 17:21)

SOWING AND REAPING
Mk. 4:26

So is the kingdom of God, as if a man should cast seed into the ground; And should sleep, and rise night and day, and the seed should spring and grow up, he knoweth not how. For the earth bringeth forth fruit of herself; first the blade, then the ear, after that the full corn in the ear. But when the fruit is brought forth, immediately he putteth in the sickle, because the harvest is come.

Know How

This parable of the kingdom describes two levels of consciousness, or knowledge, distinguishable in this manner: one is the knowledge of how to create, and the other is the knowledge of what to create. According to Jesus, man does not know how creation works. But he does know what is being created in his experience of life, or at least he should know what he sows: what he conceives, thinks, believes, says, and chooses to do and be. And though he doesn't know how It works, he does know how to work with It.

Let's not confuse not knowing how Life works for not knowing what you are to do to facilitate that work. We'll never know how from a universal perspective. Our knowledge is defined by our personal perspective. We know how to cooperate. We know what we can do, and when to do it. We know that if we sow a seed with the expectation that it grow and bear fruit, then we had better attend to it: water, cultivate, etc. We know that if we intentionally sow a seed of thought then we must be attentive, alert and aware of the ways in which we can nurture and facilitate a greater awareness of that which we have conceived. And if we pay attention, we need not be surprised, or chagrined.

In an individual, know-how refers to what they have learned through experience, trial and error, and the repeated application of a principle. On a universal basis, know-how is the creative ability of Life Itself. Life knows how to create, while man knows only what he would like to see created. For a man, know-how instructs our choices. For Life, know-how is creative Self-expression. Everyone has an idea of what they would choose to have, do, or be, but only Life has the knowledge and ability to get the job done properly.

To prosper from this knowledge, we must also know when to do the work of acceptance. We have to know when the harvest has come. The time is right when the fruit is ripe. We must be able to recognize the seed in the fruit. We must be able to recognize in our experience of life what we've expressed of our life, and accept it. When we see the nature, the essence, of what we've given in what we have to accept, the harvest is ready for us. The kingdom of heaven is like a man who knows what to expect and when to accept. He doesn't know how. He knows only what and when. And, since we are continuously sowing seeds, and Life is constantly growing, there is always something ready for harvest. There is always something for us to accept, and the time for that is always now. As Emerson put it: "The lesson which these observations convey is, Be, and not seem. Let us acquiesce. Let us take our bloated nothingness out of the path of the divine circuits. Let us unlearn our wisdom of the world. Let us lie low in the Lord's power and learn that truth alone makes rich and great."

Consciousness

In this parable of the kingdom, Jesus did not say that the kingdom is like a man, or seed, the ground into which the seed is sown, or the fruit of the earth that comes forth. The kingdom is likened to all of these elements, working together in a creative process, but the kingdom is not the process. Jesus did not say that

God's kingdom was simply the creativity of Nature. He did not compare the kingdom to seeds blowing in the wind and growing wild in the fields, but he often compared it to sowing and reaping. The description of the kingdom is not complete with the sequence of seed, blade, ear, and corn. Until the man puts forth the sickle, harvesting the fruit of his labors and Life's creativity, the kingdom is not realized

Cooperation

Creativity is a constant, a given, a fact of reality. Jesus made a distinction between this impersonal operation of Life and our cooperation with Its Laws. The kingdom of God is like a man who cooperates with what is going on in life, and works with It to his advantage. The fact that seeds become plants that bear fruit does not define a heavenly state. It is a fact of Life. Our awareness of this fact, and of how Life works and how we might cooperate with It, that is a blessed state. That is heaven, and that is all there is to it. Heaven is our consciousness of living and working in harmony with God, using Its principles to prosper our experience of Life. In reality, creativity and abundance exist without man's participation or cooperation, and this is the reality that many people suffer within: the reality of not participating or cooperating with Life.

Participation

The kingdom of God is that experience of reality in which we participate and cooperate with Life, prospering in the process. Again, the kingdom is not a process, but rather it is our conscious participation in the process. The kingdom is not only the realm of God's Law, but also our abiding within and living by that Law. The kingdom of God is not a place. It is a dynamic state in which transformation brings forth abundance. Our experience of the kingdom of God is the creative consciousness through which we express and experience Life. We enter into the kingdom to the degree that we realize that the Life of God is the creative force, the abundant source, and realizing It, consciously work with It.

There is not much that we need to know in order to cooperate with this process. Our participation amounts to:

1.   Sowing the seed.
2.   Tending to the field night and day.
3.   Reaping the harvest.

The first step is simply broadcasting our seeds of thought, our concepts, beliefs and ideas. We do this constantly. It is not second nature; it is our primary nature to think, to conceive, to imagine and express ourselves intelligently. All of that is going on in the background while we give our attention to everything else we do. We go through the day broadcasting our thought to Life. It need not be done with care, a ritual, a formula or in any special state of mind. We don't need to know how to think or what to think in order to fulfill the first requirement of working with Life: Think! Express yourself!

Faith

We don't need to know how things grow, how Life works, what is going on in the soil, in the unseen process of Life. We don't need to know how. In fact, we are better off not knowing — or thinking that we know how. When we think we know how, we just get in the way. We delay. We complicate. There is nothing wrong with knowing how Life works; however, thinking that we know enough to do the creative work ourselves creates another set of problems. However, it would be a mistake to not act on what we do know in deference to what we don't know. Even though we don't know how It works, we may work with It, if we have faith that It does work.

Faith doesn't make It work. Our faith puts us to work. With faith, we attend to our business with patience and certainty, assured of results in due time. An enlightened mind combines the knowledge of how best to work with Life's creative intelligence, and the understanding of when and how to get out of Its way.

SEED IN THE FIELD
Mt. 13:24

The kingdom of heaven is likened unto a man which sowed
good seed in his field:

Heaven

The content of this verse is usually ignored, because the verses
that follow tell the parable of the wheat and tares. That is a much
more interesting story. It addresses the question of good seed and
weed seed, the desirable and undesirable, positive and negative
thoughts, and what to do about it. But we shouldn't overlook Jesus
description of heaven in our hurry to find out what to do about our
thinking.

God's kingdom (heaven) is like good seed in a field. Jesus
describes heaven as a creative process that reproduces abundantly.
Heaven is not a place but a process. It is a state of mind we enter
into, but it is also an inner state of awareness and consciousness.
We are within it, in the sense that we work with it, and it is within
us in the sense that it works through us. But, in no sense is heaven
a place or location.

The notion that one must die to get to heaven is nonsense.
Heaven is a state of being, a working relationship. I'm reminded of
lyrics from the song Freedom, from the musical, Shenandoah, by
Geld and Udell. It is a song about the distinction between escaping
slavery and being free.

Freedom ain't a state like Maine or Virginia.
Freedom ain't across some county line.
Freedom is a flame that burns within ya,
Freedom's in the state of mind.

It is easy to confuse the essence of freedom with conditions in
which it occurs, but if we did that, we'd continue to chase after

116

those conditions instead of facing the reality that we are free. We'd postpone our freedom until we get to some promised land, only to find when we arrive that we are no freer than we ever were. Similarly, I think it is a mistake to postpone our experience of Heaven. With apologies to Geld and Udell, I would have us sing:

Heaven ain't a kingdom up in the heavens.

Heaven ain't over here or there.

Heaven is around and within ya.

Heaven's in the state of mind.

One escapes enslavement only after realizing that we are all free. And likewise, we'll find ourselves in Heaven when we realize that we are always one with the Lord, our God; for the Law of Life is the law of our life as well. We must keep in mind that heaven is not something we can observe in the facts and conditions of the world in which we live. To see heaven, we will have to behold it within. Those who interpreted the prophecies of the Messiah literally were looking forward to heaven on earth, freedom from oppression, self-governance, and the rule of divine Law, someday. Jesus had a different kingdom in mind: And when he was demanded of the Pharisees, when the kingdom of God should come, he answered them and said, "The kingdom of God cometh not with observation: Neither shall they say, Lo here! or, lo there! for, behold, the kingdom of God is within you." (Lk. 17:20-21)

Seed and Soil

Heaven is not just a creative field, which if ignored will quickly fill with weeds. Heaven is as a field that a man sows with seed. For life to be a heavenly experience, the seed must be of our choosing. Forget the notion that you would have Heaven on Earth if only God would make it so, if only God would tell you what to think and do — and if only you would comply. You sow, and you reap what you sow, and that is as it should be. That is heaven. That is the law of Nature, and the nature of God's Law. You must reap what you sow, because the seed is a thought sown (known) within you, and the growth and fulfillment of that seed is a process that takes place within you. You reap what you sow because you experience what you express.

The soul of man has been likened to the soil of his field. Please note: the verse states that a man sowed good seeds in his field. His field is his use of the Law of Nature. His field is not separate from your field, or mine, or any place on Earth, even if he purchases it, fences it in and posts No Trespassing signs. It's all one; which is why his field is creative.

Likewise, we believe our soul to be a creative mental field, in which we sow seeds of thought, self-concepts, which become the experience we reap. Our mind is creative simply because our mind is our use of the one Mind of God. Just as a man's field is his use of Nature, our mind is our use of the creative intelligence of Life Itself. Our mind is creative, not because we will or wish it to be so, but because it is the nature of Life to create.

The only distinction between his field and mine or yours is the use we each make of the creativity within us and around us. We each get differing results because we sow different seeds in the same creative soil. And, we each get differing amounts when we sow the same seeds! The difference can be accounted for by the condition of our soil, our field, our unique use of the creativity of Life. Some poor souls have a harsh environment and more needs than they can meet; just as some soil is full of weeds and rocks. Those facts do not change the creative nature of one's mind, or the process by which we reap what we sow, but it does diminish the results. We have greater results as the soil is more nurturing, more accepting, more fertile. We harvest more when there are fewer weeds. But aside from the amount, the nature of the process is the same. It is the nature of the soil to be a creative field in which seeds are sown, nurtured, and grow to bear their fruit (more seeds). It is the nature of our soul to bring forth that which we sow within.

And aside from the condition of the soil, owing to our use or disuse of it, the nature of the soil is the same throughout — a creative medium in which seeds come to fruition. Jesus didn't say that heaven was simply the creative process of seeds sprouting up wherever they can put down roots. He didn't say that heaven was like seeds blowing in the wind, which spring up as weeds in your lawn. He said heaven was like good seed that a man chooses to sow in his own field. His words indicate that the kingdom of heaven is conscious and intentional cooperation with the Law of Life, in such a way that we gladly reap what we sow. Uprooting weeds is not a heavenly experience. Even so, getting the consequences of the choices we make is the nature of Law. To make a good choice and get consequences that are beneficial is the nature of Heaven. Conscious cooperation with the Law of Life is heaven.

WHEAT AND TARES
Mt. 13:24-30

The kingdom of heaven is likened unto a man which sowed
good seed in his field: But while men slept, his enemy came
and sowed tares among the wheat, and went his way. But when
the blade was sprung up, and brought forth fruit, then appeared
the tares also. So the servants of the householder came and said
unto him, "Sir, didst not thou sow good seed in thy field? from
whence then hath it tares?" He said unto them, "An enemy hath
done this." The servants said unto him, "Wilt thou then that we
go and gather them up?" But he said, "Nay; lest while ye
gather up the tares, ye root up also the wheat with them. Let
both grow together until the harvest: and in the time of harvest
I will say to the reapers, Gather ye together first the tares, and
bind them in bundles to burn them: but gather the wheat into
my barn."

A Paradox

If you think of heaven as a paradise, then paradise is a paradox.
Paradise is a walled garden, a sanctuary, a park set off from the rest
of the world, safe and secure for its inhabitants. That could also
describe a prison farm, but paradise is usually a reference to the
Garden of Eden. Those who think of heaven as paradise long for a
return to that garden. But the way this parable describes heaven
presents a paradox. Weeding the garden is not what most people
think of as a heavenly experience, yet Jesus thought of it like that.
His parable presents what at first appears to be a problem (weeds)
as an opportunity to resolve the actual problem (prejudice).
Perhaps all of Jesus' parables are paradoxes; not just analogies and
allegory, but a contradiction of what we believe to be true.

If we take away the analogy, the kingdom of heaven is like the experience of a man who thinks good thoughts, only to discover that his mind contains not only that which he intended, but that which he did not intend as well. He would like to reap only what he has sown and avoid unintended consequences of thoughts implanted by others, but he cannot easily distinguish one from the other. He cannot judge which concepts will bear fruit, and which will be fruitless, prior to seeing the evidence. If he attempts to pre-judge the outcome, either judging by appearances or by experience, he will undoubtedly uproot some of the wheat and leave some of the tares. He faces a dilemma: accept them both, or reject them both. The problem is that when we cannot see what to do or what not to do, and we don't know what to choose, we tend to do as we've always done and choose as we usually do. Making a judgment based on prior judgments, without the benefit of know what you are looking at, is prejudice. It would be an act of prejudice to attempt to weed out the bad seed when you cannot distinguish the good from the bad, the right from wrong, one from another. Being a man of faith, he chooses instead to keep an open mind, waiting for proof (or the lack thereof) in order to evaluate the worth of his thoughts. Eventually, some thoughts will bear fruit and some will not. He can then accept the good and completely reject that which is not so good.

Now, reconsider the parable of the Wheat and Tares, with its paradoxical nature in mind.

Householder / Servants

Jesus designated the man as a householder. The house is where he lives, but more pertinently, it is where his word is law. He is in the position of decision-maker, the head of the house. He rules the house, or rather his rules determine what goes on in the house. His house is his castle. He describes it, and it defines him. Being the householder means that the house and everything it holds belongs to him, including the servants. They are his. They are there to serve his will. He has a will, and they do not. He exercises his will, and they are willing. He has a choice, and they do not. Everyone who lives under his roof are dependent on him, and do his bidding.

It is easy to see how his position confuses and compromises his ability to relate in a loving or nurturing way with the members of his family. But, this is a parable of the kingdom of heaven, not an analysis of family dynamics. The house is the kingdom, and his kingdom is the consciousness in which he lives, moves, has his being, makes decisions and exerts his will. His servants are the qualities of thought that serve at his will. Some servants serve him well; such as Patience and Perseverance. Others do not serve as well; such as Insolence and Ignorance. The qualities of thought and attitude that make up our consciousness are our mental household, and they serve us as well as their nature allows.

Many of Jesus' parables are about servants of the king, or servants in the fields or the house. We miss the point if we think of the servants as people, or think that they represent us in the parable. To understand the parables of the kingdom we must remember where Jesus located the kingdom: "… behold, the kingdom of God is within you." (Lk. 17:21) The kingdom is within us; the household is within us, the seeds in the field and the servants are all within us. The parable describes our state of mind.

Men / Enemy

What is the enemy of men? We are our own worst enemy. There is nothing else in the universe that exists in opposition to us. But keep in mind that this is a parable of the inner kingdom of God, not a commentary on society. Therefore, the enemy within is our primary adversary, and the adversarial relationship we have with ourselves is simply our ability to stand in opposition to our self. We consider opposing points of view. We argue with our self. We struggle with the temptation to settle, to compromise, to be less and accept less than our potential. Jesus said: "Agree with thine adversary quickly, whiles thou art in the way with him;" (Mt.5:25)

Why should we agree? Why not defeat your adversary? Perhaps because that would be a self-defeating proposition! Agreement is the only way to end the adversarial relationship. There is a point we can agree upon, a point at which we are not in opposition to one another. Finding inner agreement is the first thing we should do, for the consequence of inner conflict is guilt and imprisonment. If we don't agree quickly, we will at last come back to the point where we must agree in order to be free.

Waking / Sleeping

This parable describes the state of men: we are not in agreement; not with others, and not within ourselves. We make good choices, but when inattentive, we unconsciously sow the field with weeds.

How is it that a man can sow good seed, and yet we see evidence of weeds in his field? According to the parable, the weeds were sown as the man was asleep, not conscious of what he was thinking. Perhaps he was dreaming, or day-dreaming, wishing, hoping and worrying. We are not always praying, but it seems that God is always listening.

The waking state of man is a conscious state of mind; while sleeping is an unconscious state. When conscious, our thoughts are (more or less) intentional; and unconscious thought is unintended. We are attentive when conscious (more or less) and inattentive when unconscious. Affirmations and denials, accepting and rejecting, choosing and refusing are conscious activities. The unconscious state of mind does not discriminate. It is much like the soil in that it cannot select or reject any seed. The unconscious state of mind accepts whatever one hears, and it then repeats and perpetuates it.

Can a man be held accountable for what happens unconsciously, automatically, when he is not on the job, when he is, in fact, idling away the day in speculative considerations? Yes, at least Jesus thought so: "But I say unto you, That every idle word that men shall speak, they shall give account thereof in the day of judgment. For by thy words thou shalt be justified, and by thy words thou shalt be condemned." (Mt. 12:36-37) He wasn't talking about our word in prayer, but the words we speak without benefit of conscious deliberation and intention. Every thought has creative potential; the potential to shape our self-concept and determine what we express and experience in life. We don't always wish to reap as we sow, but the soil must work with what we give it, and we must contend with even the unintended consequences of our unconscious thought.

How is it that a man can sow good seed, and yet we see evidence of weeds in his field? According to the parable, the weed seed must have been sown when the man was asleep and not conscious of what he was thinking or doing. Perhaps he was dreaming, or day-dreaming, wishing, hoping and worrying. We are not always praying, but it seems that God is always listening.

The waking state of man is a conscious state of mind; while sleeping is an unconscious state. When conscious, our thoughts are (more or less) intentional; and unconscious thought is unintended. We are attentive when conscious (more or less) and inattentive when unconscious. Affirmations and denials, accepting and rejecting, choosing and refusing are conscious activities. The unconscious state of mind is not discriminating. The unconscious state of mind is like the soil in that it cannot select or reject any seed. Whatever one says, it accepts and perpetuates.

Good Seed / Weed Seed

The good seed produces goods, that which you consider to be good or valuable. The goodness of the seed is not a matter of whether or not it is viable or productive, but whether or not it is intentional. The weed seed is just as viable and productive, but it is not as good because it does not produce the intended results. The comparison is not between good and bad, but intentional and unintentional, or perhaps that is the only difference between that which we call good or bad.

In the parable, the servants questioned the quality of the seed used to sow the field. It is considered good seed if not contaminated with the seeds of weeds. Even today, a bag of grass seed will contain a list of all the types of seed in the bag. The lower the percentage of noxious weed seed, the better the quality. But there is also the question of how much of the seed is perennial and how much is annual. The annual varieties grow quickly but last for only one season. If you don't wish to plant a lawn every year, you'll desire a higher percentage of perennial seed. It is considered to be of better quality and costs more, but it is worth it.

Wheat / Tares

Some translations of this parable refer to wheat and weeds, but it is thought that the weed they had in mind was the tare plant: a rye grass that looks much like wheat in the early stages of growth. In a wheat field, a tare is a weed that can't be weeded out. But at harvest, the fruits of the wheat are evident, and the tare can be easily identified as something less desirable. The point of the parable is this: you can't waste your time trying to uproot the unintended and undesirable. You can't always tell the difference between the good seed and the weed. Don't worry about the fact that some of the seed you sow will never bear fruit. Harvest the good that you can and discard the rest.

Resolution / Problem

It is rare that we find a bag of seed that is 100% of what you intend to sow, and even more rare to find a consciousness that is

100% positive, affirmative, desirable, beneficial and true. It should come as no surprise that there are weeds in the field. The only question is what to do about them.

The parable prescribes a resolution to the problem of weeds in the wheat field. Weeds are a problem in that they reduce the value of the harvest. Instead of 100% good seed, the field may produce 50% good seed and 50% weed seed. The same work and effort produce half of what it could. This problem is compounded by the fact that the servants can't pull out the weeds without also uprooting the wheat because we cannot distinguish between wheat and tare, good and not so good — until the wheat bears fruit, and we can see the results. Remember what Jesus said: "Ye shall know them by their fruits. Do men gather grapes of thorns, or figs of thistles?" (Mt.7:16)

We'd like to think that we can judge by appearances, or reason sufficiently to know the truth of the matter, but we can't. The only way to know it is true is to prove it. Show me the proof! We cannot approve of it until we see the proof of it. If you prove it then it must be true. If you can't prove it, then it is less likely to be true. It may or may not be true, but either way, until proven, it has no value for you. All problems are resolved at harvest, when the results make it clear as to what is the good seed, and what is not. The good seed is that which we sow with intention; the weed is the unintentional concept. The good seed was a conscious choice; the weed was an unconscious choice. The good seed bears fruit; the weed does not. Or rather, the good seed bears the fruit we intended, while the weed has unintended, and therefore unacceptable, consequences.

Henry David Thoreau defended the weed as a flower whose virtue is not yet known. It is not that a weed has no virtue, no value, or is good for nothing. We simply don't know what its virtue is. If it is not as we intended, we reject it. We often encounter this situation in our lives: The waiter brings a dish we did not order. Do

126

we eat it or send it back? If the giver is thoughtful, the gift is given with a receipt, so that we can take it back and get whatever we choose. When we plant a flower garden, we weed out all the grasses, herbs, vegetables and trees that manage to take root. All these 'weeds' have value, somewhere, to someone, but not here and now. We expect to reap as we sow, to get as good as we've given, and nothing less, nothing else, is acceptable. Good and bad are relative terms. There are no good or bad seeds, except our thinking makes it so. It grows one as well as the other, and often the 'weed' grows better.

Kingdom of Heaven

Some teach that a heavenly garden is waiting, out there somewhere, but I don't believe it, and I don't think Jesus thought of it that way. According to his parables and statements, the kingdom of heaven is an inner experience, an inner field of consciousness, in which we sow seeds of thought every day; some intentionally and some not so. We would like to think that we can tell the difference between a good idea and that which is not so good, but we can't. The only way to tell the true from the false, the fact from the fiction, is to let it all stand side by side and see what good comes of it. Only time will tell. When we see the results, then we shall know what is productive and valuable, and what is a waste of time and space.

A NET
Mt. 13:47-52

Again, the kingdom of heaven is like unto a net, that was cast into the sea, and gathered of every kind: Which, when it was full, they drew to shore, and sat down, and gathered the good into vessels, but cast the bad away.

So shall it be at the end of the world: the angels shall come forth, and sever the wicked from among the just, And shall cast them into the furnace of fire: there shall be wailing and gnashing of teeth.

Jesus saith unto them, Have ye understood all these things? They say unto him, Yea, Lord. Then said he unto them, Therefore every scribe which is instructed unto the kingdom of heaven is like unto a man that is an householder, which bringeth forth out of his treasure things new and old.

Have Ye Understood?

These six verses are usually considered as a whole, but they are three separate analogies — fishing, judging, housekeeping — set in place as one parable of the kingdom of heaven. All three have a common theme, which tends to warrant presenting them in such a way that the next verse explains the previous verse. Those who are satisfied with a literal reading of these verses might accept that sorting through a catch of fish is meant to describe how angels are going to judge people on Judgment Day, the day when God cleans house, sorting out the old and new.

Parables

I think it unlikely that Jesus ever presented these analogies of the kingdom in this sequence of verses. A parable is a teaching device. Its purpose is to allow the listener to search within until they grasp an inner awareness. One who teaches through parables would not address the question (What is the kingdom of heaven like?), by providing three answers to his own question. He might raise the same question three times, in a slightly different guise each time, to provide the listener with more to work with, but he wouldn't provide three answers to the same question. He couldn't if they were answers, rather than questions designed to prod us to a deeper understanding. A parable does not include an explanation for those who can't fathom the hidden meaning. Statements about the end of the world and treasures old and new are offered as an explanation of the parable of the net.

There are many instances when Jesus did give his disciples a private explanation of his public teachings. The disciples were depicted as either needing tutoring because they were slow to understand, or because they had the unique relationship of student to teacher. While Jesus could lecture to the twelve; he couldn't manage a class of thousands, so the multitude got the study questions. If that is the case, then we should be grateful that a disciple wrote down the explanations, saving us the trouble of pondering the parables, but again, I don't think that is the case in these verses.

Prophecy

Here a parable is followed with a prophecy of the end of the world; which is neither a parable or an explanation of the parable, unless the parable is about the end of the world. If that is the case, if Jesus is saying that the kingdom of heaven comes as the end of the world, then this parable is at odds with the rest of the parables and other tenants of his teachings. For example, Lk. 17:20-21 clearly describes God's kingdom as a spiritual state of being, that we need only recognize within us to realize around and about us.

Apocalyptic

It is difficult for me to reconcile these two views of God's kingdom: one an inner kingdom you can behold within you, with the other that is an end to the world as we know it. The pattern of linking prophecies of the end of the world with a parable of the kingdom also occurs in the Gospel of Matthew, chapter 13: 36-43. And in Matthew, chapter 25, verses 31 - 46 we find a description of the end of the world; but these verses stand alone, in that they do not continue the parable. While the verses are attributed to Jesus, they are inconsistent with the body of his teachings; which leads me to agree with those Bible scholars who consider the apocalyptic verses in the Gospels to be attributed to Jesus, but not contributed by Jesus.

In the gospel of Matthew, we find the kingdom of prophecy conflated with the kingdom of parables. Those verses may be well-intentioned attempts to explain Jesus' teachings by including popular prophecies of the apocalypse: a divine intervention that would end servitude and suffering, ushering in a return to the past glory of the kingdom of Israel. That 'earthly kingdom' is what the majority of Jews longed for, not the heavenly kingdom. Or such verses could simply be an effort to claim the endorsement of Jesus for prophecies about the end of their suffering. Regardless of their intentions, their methods and inclusions are suspect. The verses about the end of the world and gnashing teeth (Mt. 13:49-50) are not a parable, nor an explanation of the parables that precede and follow these verses. It is simply an endorsement of a prophecy, inserted into the narrative.

Questions

Parables are supposed to raise questions about scriptures, and also about our view of reality. So, we might consider the role of a parable to raise this question: What does that mean for me? In these verses we find three descriptions of the kingdom of heaven, each of which prompts us to question our understanding of the king, the kingdom, and of heaven.

King

While it was an accepted fact that the king was Herod, or someone of his lineage, there was a prophecy of a king arising out of the lineage of one of the old kings, David. People went to great lengths, before and after his crucifixion, to attribute this kingship to Jesus. Some did it in support of him, others as an accusation against him. Most conflated these prophecies of a savior king with those of the Messiah, the Christ, and while Jesus claimed to be the Christ and to have fulfilled the prophecies of the Messiah, he had a new idea of King. He never claimed to be the king of Heaven, or on Earth. It was God's kingdom, and the King was the Lord, our God, our Father, which art in heaven.

Kingdom

Jesus kept talking about kings and kingdoms in his parables to get people to question their view of reality. Is the kingdom of God a geopolitical state, or the realm of God's Law? Is the kingdom he spoke of the land that the Israelites conquered and then lost to greater empires, or was he speaking of a spiritual state? The prophecies of the kingdom were widely understood to be a forecast of a brighter future for the Jews who were living in subjugation to foreign rulers. The prophecies could also be a prediction of war, rebellion, and hell on Earth followed by heaven on Earth. Those who asked when God's kingdom would come were asking for a date on the calendar. Jesus might have well responded: When do you think? He said that we cannot see it coming, but we can behold within us the kingdom of God. He believed that was the true fulfillment of a proper understanding of prophecy.

End Times

Even those who rejected the notion of rebellion against the Roman Empire still looked for a quasi-spiritual version of the same thing, someday: a war of good against evil, where God's kingdom would be restored on Earth, with Jesus as king. It was considered to be the end of the world, the end of the world as they knew it. Self-righteous radicals longed for the day when they are judged, and awarded with heaven on Earth. On the other side of the issue, the religious establishment was afraid that Jesus was just such a radical because he was preaching to those who believed in a Judgment Day and an earthly kingdom. He was asking them to think of the kingdom as something that was not only at hand, but within their grasp now.

Those who consider prophecies to be a literal prediction misunderstand the language of prophecy, and they misconstrue the parables of the kingdom if they considered them to be a prediction of a global event, a divine intervention by God. While predictions and prophecy are about the future, parables are about the present.

Many thought an apocalypse was imminent and quoted Jesus' parables as endorsing their expectations. It was not an imminent event, and for the nearly three thousand years since the kingdom of Israel fell apart, the kingdom of God has never been and never will be imminent. On the other hand, the kingdom Jesus was talking about has always been present: immanent but not imminent.

Inner Kingdom

How confusing that the kingdom of Israel is considered to be the kingdom of God, and the kingdom of heaven is considered to be Gods kingdom as well. Jesus made it clear that his kingdom was not of this world, but that was not enough to clear up the confusion for those who wished to align their idea of the kingdom with Biblical prophecies. Even though thousands of years go by, and countless predictions of the end date are proven to be erroneous, the faithful remain patient and consider the possibility that Thy kingdom will come any day now. That may be a fine attitude to take, but it is not the approach to Life that Jesus took.

For Jesus, God is spirit, and God's kingdom is a spiritual state, a state of being at one with God. He taught that we can realize our oneness with God, right here and right now. Others pushed the date of that realization off into the indefinite future, perhaps after one dies. Whether it was a belief in resurrection or ascension into the heavens, neither view reflected Jesus' teaching that the kingdom of God is within us. His teaching was not that it would be any day now but that the kingdom of God was and is now!

Choice

As noted earlier, these verses depict a common theme: a choice is being made. Fishermen are sorting out their catch. Angels are sorting out good and evil. The head of the house is sorting out his inventory of old and new. The kingdom of heaven is being likened to standing at the point of choice, knowing that you have a choice, and making that choice. That choice is the essence of freedom, and the realization of one's freedom is a heavenly state of mind. Mt. 13:47-48, and Mt. 13:52, are about whether or not one is conscious of their freedom.

Although Mt. 13:49-50 is also about choosing, the choice is out of our hands. These verses speak of a consequence, not a choice. They describe divine judgment, not spiritual freedom. Ironically, the role of good judgment is to facilitate choice between two or more perceived options, but when people are objects of judgment it is to facilitate choosing for them, and often to impose punishment in addition to the consequences that accompanied their choices.

- I'd rather be free to suffer (or enjoy) the consequences of my choices, than judged and punished (or rewarded) for the choices I made.
- I'd rather think of myself as a fisherman than a fish caught in a net.
- I'd rather think of the kingdom of heaven as a realm of freedom under Law, than a court of judgment.

Fishing

The first of the two parables describes our mind as a net that indiscriminately gathers in the desirable and the undesirable fish. The sea is often an analogy for consciousness because of its unseen depths, and for the unpredictable way in which it can change from calm to turbulent. It is analogous to an emotional state of mind, in which we try to stay afloat, keeping our head above water, if not consciously rising above it. Just as we must sort the fish that we net, we must sort through our thoughts and feelings in such a way that we keep the valuable (true) and discard the rest (false). The person who knows this, and does this, has a level of freedom not enjoyed by those who live at the mercy of their consciousness alone. A person who is free is not without unintended thoughts and emotions, for our mind casts a broad net, and we get what we get. The free person is the one who chooses what to remain conscious of and what to forgive and forget, and, therefore, how to feel, and what to be.

Equating the inner kingdom of heaven with one's consciousness is a common misperception. A heavenly spiritual state cannot be represented by the unfathomable sea, nor the fish that swim in it, or the net — the unthinking, indiscriminate, consciousness that gathers in all. The kingdom of heaven is a conscious state of being focused on the good, on the nature of God. I am reminded of the apostle Paul's advice: "… whatsoever things are true; whatsoever things are honest, whatsoever things are just, whatsoever things are pure, whatsoever things are lovely, whatsoever things are of good report; if there be any virtue, and if there be any praise, think on these things." (Phl. 4:8)

Housekeeping

Like the fisherman, the householder needs to sort through what he has. We live within our consciousness; that is our house. As a conscious being, we are responsible for our consciousness. Our role is to determine what to keep, what to treasure, what has value. We have to choose, from amongst the old and the new, that which is true. It is hell to not know what to do, what to think, what to believe when your mind is full of conflicting thoughts, unresolved issues, and worthless old stuff. As the head of your household, it is up to you to choose. But you can't choose between the old and new if you know only the old ways, or only new ways.

Remember, Jesus did not reject the Old Testament, the old ways and traditions or the old prophecies. He intended to fulfill the promise of the old, in a new way. He did not reject his faith and establish a new religion based upon himself. Others did that. He sought to perfect his faith in his religious beliefs. He saw the value in those teachings, and chose to become the embodiment of the truths he found in them. His teachings were indeed a rich blend of old and new thoughts.

The learned person, the scribe instructed in the kingdom of heaven, has a choice to make. We are scribes instructed in the kingdom of heaven. We know how to read the Law, and write it in our heart and mind. We have a household ledger, an inventory that takes into account all that we hold to be true. Being accountable is what makes us a householder. Understanding the nature of the kingdom of heaven, the principles of God's Law, and the parables Jesus taught, we have criteria by which we can evaluate what we have in mind, holding onto that which has value and discarding the rest. Choosing that which is good, valuable and true, bringing order to our life and establishing peace of mind, this is living in the kingdom of heaven.

SOWING SEEDS
Mt. 13:3-9

Behold, a sower went forth to sow; And when he sowed, some seeds fell by the way side, and the fowls came and devoured them up: Some fell upon stony places, where they had not much earth: and forthwith they sprung up, because they had no deepness of earth: And when the sun was up, they were scorched; and because they had no root, they withered away. And some fell among thorns; and the thorns sprung up, and choked them: But other fell into good ground, and brought forth fruit, some an hundredfold, some sixtyfold, some thirtyfold. Who hath ears to hear, let him hear.

A Sower

In answer to the disciples request for an explanation (see Mt. 13:13-19), Jesus described the sower as anyone who hears the word of the kingdom. Whether or not one who hears is also one who understands is another matter. Jesus considered his teachings to be a blessing for those people who were able to hear and understand them. More than once, he rebuked his disciples for their lack of understanding.

- "… perceive ye not yet, neither understand? have ye your heart yet hardened? Having eyes, see ye not? and having ears, hear ye not?" (Mk. 8:17)

Who hath eyes to see, and ears to hear? It is only one who understands that truly sees or hears.

- "For this people's heart is waxed gross, and *their* ears are dull of hearing, and their eyes they have closed; lest at any time they should see with *their* eyes, and hear with *their* ears, and should understand with *their* heart, and should be converted, and I should heal them." (Mt. 13:15)

The sower has not only heard, but also understood, thus sowing in mind the words Jesus spoke about the kingdom of God. However, for the seed to be of any value it must bear fruit, and for one's word to be of any value it must be expressed in one's actions. The sower has good seeds to sow; but will anything come of it? James the Just (the brother of Jesus, who succeeded Jesus as the leader of the early Christian church) made a comment in one of his letters that addresses this point: "But be ye doers of the word, and not hearers only, deceiving your own selves." (Jas. 1:22)

Seeds

Sowing seed is one means through which Life finds abundant self-expression. And like seed in the soil, thought in mind has the potential to enrich our life. In the parable, the sower is a listener, a thinker, a hearer of the word; which makes the idea in his mind analogous to a seed, the seed of thought: "… that which was sown in his heart." (Mt. 13:19) In nature, sowing the seed is an act of conception that gives expression to Life, and similarly, a thought in mind becomes a self-concept. An idea, belief, or self-concept is a seed of thought through which we express and experience our life. Our thinking begins this inner creative process if and when it is an act of conception resulting in self-expression. Remember: be ye doers of the word, and not hearers only.

Seeds are creative because it is the nature of Life to be creative, and It finds expression through them. Our words are creative only as Life finds expression through them. If our words, thoughts and concepts are devoid of understanding, they do not allow for the expression of Life. Words that do not express or inspire understanding are no more seeds of thought than an empty shell is a seed.

Life is expressed and experienced through the concepts we have in mind. The "word of the kingdom" that Jesus spoke of is just such a concept. It is an awareness of the presence of God within us, and it is the understanding of how to live and work with It. It is a seed of thought which when sown in mind, may bear fruit. That is the nature of the seeds we have to sow, and we have to account for those that do not grow.

The Wayside

Some seeds of thought which we intend to sow never get to where they are supposed to go. They end up by the wayside. Why? It is primarily because we discard them. If our seed is not carefully sown in the field, if it is carelessly broadcast, scattered far and wide, then some seed will end up by the wayside as food for the birds. In Jesus' time, fields were planted by the broadcast method. Invariably, some seeds fell beyond the tilled soil. They fell by the wayside. Fortunately, some would fall on good ground too.

For a seed to be a part of the creative process, it must be sown, released, cast forth; we've got to drop it. Likewise, for the seed of thought to fulfill its creative potential, we must release it from the conscious hold we have upon it. It must come to rest at a sub-conscious, subjective and receptive, level of mind. A seed in the hand is not creative. We must sow the seed for it to be creative, and likewise, the seed of thought must be released to the soul. We release the seed by letting go, and that would work for a seed of thought too, if only we would let go of it. Once we've grasped it fully, we have to let it go if it is to grow. As good as it is, we have to drop it. Letting go requires faith in the creative process.

At the conclusion of prayer we say Amen, and so it is, and so I let it be, and so on; but if we go on and on about it there can be no conscious release, and no subjective acceptance. We are supposed to turn our attention back to life and living and go about our business. But some thoughts are so good, so promising, so

139

important to us that we won't let go of them. The idea we wish to accept, we remain conscious of, and that is a mistake. Make no mistake, we must release the seed of thought from conscious consideration. It must be sown in the mental field of the creative intelligence of Life Itself. Just as a seed is released to the soil, our thought in prayer must be released to the Soul of Life in order to begin the creative process. There it is accepted and embodied as a quality of our consciousness. It is only at a subjective level of our consciousness that an idea has any influence on the creative process, for the creative quality of mind functions only at this subjective level of thought where all ideas are accepted as valid.

Again, the analogy of a seed is valid. If the seed stays on the surface of the soil, it does not survive, and if an idea remains a conscious consideration, it has no role in the creative process. It is sidelined by conscious considerations while creativity takes place in the unseen depths of consciousness. There it is incorporated, becoming part of our belief system, a pattern of thought through which Life finds expression.

Ironically, when finally we get it, we must forget it in order to fulfill the potential of the idea. As long as the question remains unresolved, or an idea is misunderstood, it remains a conscious consideration. As we continue to ponder the possibilities, we question our confidence. We cross examine and find fault with our prayerful testimony. Usually at this point, the seed of thought is dismissed, discarded, rejected as unacceptable, unbelievable. It ends up by the wayside because we didn't accept it, and we were not able to accept it because we never released it from our conscious deliberations. Well, never is an overstatement. That which we do not consciously accept, we eventually reject.

Birds

The fowls are our foul thoughts, polluting our mental atmosphere with doubt, fear, insecurity, anger — a judgmental attitude which negates the benefit we might otherwise gain from hearing the word of the kingdom. When seeds of thought are not well received, before having a chance to take root, they are often devoured: judged, criticized and negated. In a similar manner, judgmental thinking considers the argument against as well as for the kingdom of God. It is a consideration of the negative as well as the positive. It finds fault, pointing out the bad for each good, wrong for each right, and no for each yes. Self-judgment, in that we argue with and demean ourselves, negates the positive and leaves us with nothing in mind. We hear, but understand not; or should I say, understand naught. People who try to make up their minds by a process of on the one hand ... but on the other hand ... are left empty-handed.

- "When any one heareth the word of the kingdom, and understandeth *it* not, then cometh the wicked *one*, and catcheth away that which was sown in his heart. This is he which received seed by the way side." (Mt. 13:19)

[Note: The King James translation of the Bible indicates the words that the translators inserted into the text by printing them in Italics. Most English translations after the King James simply include the inserted words as if they were part of the original text. Most of the time, the italicized words are necessary grammatical insertions, but I'm of the opinion that in rare instances this affects the meaning of the verse. Try reading the verse without the inserted words, and see what you think.]

Stoney Places

It is easy to grow flowers, vegetables and herbs when the soil is one or two feet deep, but if you dig only one or two inches before you hit rocks and gravel then gardening is just an exercise in frustration. You can't grow a large flower in a small pot, and you can't grow a tall plant in a shallow plot. There must be some depth for the roots to take hold. The stony places don't provide this. They are not devoid of soil; they just don't have enough depth. You can cast seeds onto stony soil, and they may sprout up quickly, but it is because they have devoted little time and space to developing roots. They will blow over in a storm or wither in the sun. For a seed to be well rooted there must be a sufficient depth to the soil; and, for an idea to be well embodied there must be a sufficient depth of understanding, consciousness, knowledge and self-awareness. Only as we are able to dig deep will we be able to withstand the ever changing conditions and circumstances of our life.

- "But he that received the seed into stony places, the same is he that heareth the word, and anon with joy receiveth it; Yet hath he not root in himself, but dureth for a while: for when tribulation or persecution ariseth because of the word, by and by he is offended." (Mt.13:20-21)

When we find ourselves between a rock and a hard place, there is usually a willingness to listen, but we do not have the time for an in-depth consideration or deliberation. We make a choice, but not whole-heartedly. A person in this state of mind is quick to agree to the promise of a new thought. They gladly embrace the new belief only to find that they can't sustain their enthusiasm for it. Why? They do not fully understand what they have agreed to. The stoney places represent this lack of understanding — a shallowness which could result from an emotional blind spot, prejudice, pride, familiarity, or even religious convictions. Most belief systems cannot withstand an in depth examination, for most of our beliefs are not rooted in spiritual awareness but in agreement with and endorsement of the reasoning and testimony of others. It is one thing to believe in someone else and quite a different thing to believe in what they believe. Most Christians believe in Jesus, and if you ask them why they profess a belief in his teachings they will tell you that it is because they believe in Jesus. Their belief amounts to endorsing what another, or many others, said they believe. Agreement is a good way to get along with others, but it is a hard stony row to hoe as you try to make your own garden grow.

Thorns

Even a rose has thorns, and so we come to expect and accept that for every benefit there is a tax; with every light there is an accompanying shadow; for every right, there is wrong; for every gain, a little bit is lost. That is just common sense, until we confuse one for the other. When dependency is thought to be security, we have a problem. When need and want take the place of desire and require, we have a problem. When need (a mental weed) supplants love (an intentional seed), we soon wish to be free from this needy love. The idea of loving others can become entangled and confused with needing others, wanting others, trying to manipulate others. Then it seems the only alternative is to not care, and in despair we forsake people and care only for things. We take care of things, take care of business, and to a degree we take care of ourselves, but the idea of love withers away.

- "He also that received seed among the thorns is he that heareth the word; and the care of this world, and the deceitfulness of riches, choke the word, and he becometh unfruitful." (Mt.13:22)

Taking care is not the equivalent of giving love. The words and concepts, though closely related are not synonymous; they are confused. The problem lies in taking (not giving). The thorny plant is a weed that takes all the space, the sun and rain, but gives no fruit that is of value to anyone. The weeds choke the life out of the seeds we plant. The loving express themselves, and share the fruits of their life freely. The loving are fruitful; the needy are not. The thing we need take care of is that we do not become unfruitful.

The needy give only to get, but loving is not bartering. Love is a relationship of equality, but it is not an exchange. A loving relationship is only possible for those who recognizes one another as equals. In a relationship of equality, one gives for the joy of it,

143

for the good of it; not out of any need or want of a gift. Sometimes the giving is reciprocated, but it need not be. A good plant bears and shares its fruit because it is fruitful. The loving bear and share the fruits of their love because they are loving; not because it will get them anything.

Good Ground

The only seed that grows to bear fruit is the seed sown in fertile, receptive, nurturing environment which supports and sustains growth: the "good ground." Since we are planting ideas, this field must be the creative intelligence of Life Itself. It is the Mind of God in which we live and move and have our being. The good ground is the spiritual soil, the soul, through which the creative process works to bring "that which was sown in his heart" to fruition.

This parable explains that conditions in the field are a determining factor in whether or not we reap as we sow. It is never as easy as it sounds. It is not a simple matter to sow and reap. All of us have at times prayed in vain. Not every affirmation has been confirmed by our demonstration, and not every thought has become something we can grasp. There are mental conditions we must contend with: birds, rock hard ground, weeds, the heat of the moment, etc. But there is also good ground: the receptive, accepting state of mind in which an idea grows to fruition.

- "But he that received seed into the good ground is he that heareth the word, and understandeth *it*; which also beareth fruit, and bringeth forth, some an hundredfold, some sixty, some thirty." (Mt.13:23)

The fruit of any idea is the knowledge we gain from it, the insight that accompanies the embodiment of it, and the wisdom gained in bringing that idea forth. It is understanding that enriches our life, and wisdom prospers it. As the proverb says, "get wisdom, and with all thy getting get understanding." (Pr. 4:7)

144

When we think of sowing and reaping, we imagine that we lose the seed we let loose of, and that we gain whatever we can gather in. We don't seem to mind the loss of one thing if we gain something else that is greater. However, the loss and gain are one and the same. In fact, we have lost nothing, but this does not mean that we have gained nothing. The seed we lost sight of is within us. And, it is not by gathering in, but bringing forth that which we have within, that we prosper our life. It is the knowledge deeply rooted within us that prospers us, and the fruits of ideas we behold in our heart that enrich us.

We tend to think of a bountiful harvest as gathering in as much as we can get our hands on, as much as we can wrap our arms around, but the harvest will be only as much as we have been able to wrap our mind around, as much as we have embodied and embraced as acceptable, good and true. The irony is that when we sow the seed within, we reap not what we can gather in but that which we can bring forth. It is in the expression of knowledge that we experience the value and good of it. James the Just, one of Jesus' brothers and leader of the faithful after the crucifixion of Jesus, advised: "But be ye doers of the word, and not hearers only, deceiving your own selves." (Jas 1:22) In hearing the word of the kingdom, the seed of thought is sown within us, and in doing as much as we understand and are inspired to do, we reap as we have sown.

How great is that the harvest? Whether a thirty, sixty, or hundredfold return, it is a good return on our investment. With any insight, we get what we can give of it, as much as we can express of it, all that we can share and put to good use. How much is not a factor of how much we get, but how much we give. One seed produces many fold returns, but it must be brought forth from within you to be experienced by you. You have to express the love within you to know the love within you. How much love can you have? As much as you express, you can experience; and no more. I am reminded of the wisdom of Solomon on this point:

- Happy is the man that findeth wisdom, and the man that getteth understanding. For the merchandise of it is better than the merchandise of silver, and the gain thereof than fine gold. She is more precious than rubies: and all the things thou canst desire are not to be compared unto her. Length of days is in her right hand; and in her left hand riches and honour. Her ways are ways of pleasantness, and all her paths are peace. She is a tree of life to them that lay hold upon her: and happy is every one that retaineth her. (Pr.3:13-18)

Point of View Review

In theory, we get an idea, understand it, and bring forth the fruits of it, but a good theory does not guarantee good results. Good seed doesn't stand much of a chance when it must contend with birds (judgment), stoney places (shallow mindedness) and weeds (dependency). The conditions on the ground, and of the ground, will determine the results. Whether it is to be 0 or 30 fold or 60 fold or 100 fold, the results depend upon our state of mind: how well grounded we are in Life.

If you are wondering how the garden would grow if you were the sower in the parable, complete the following quiz. Your score will indicate what you have to contend with when sowing seeds of thought. Take note of all the phrases that complete the sentence stem in a way that expresses your belief. Choose each phrase you recognize as your belief.

- You can choose more than one phrase for we often have more than one belief about the topic.
- You may choose conflicting statements for we often have conflicting beliefs.

- You may also select the phrases that remind you of a long forgotten belief; for our beliefs function even when we are not conscious of them.
- Do not select an old belief which you have consciously resolved by replacing it with a new concept.

I sometimes think that…
   (a) God loves me.
   (b) God judges me.
   (c) God controls me.
   (d) God is beyond me.

My knowledge of love leads me to believe…
   (a) I am loved.
   (b) I love others when they deserve it.
   (c) I need their love.
   (d) Love begets love.

I am healthy when…
   (a) I am whole in body and soul.
   (b) the doctor says I am.
   (c) I get what my body needs.
   (d) I feel good and have no pain.

The people in my life…
   (a) are free to live as they choose.
   (b) are good and bad.
   (c) are out of control.
   (d) are the source of my good.

My spouse is…
   (a) a perfect choice for me.
   (b) a problem.

(c) is my better half.

(d) my most valued asset.

Children ...

    (a) love me.

    (b) judge me.

    (c) need me.

    (d) tax me.

My friends...

    (a) love and respect me.

    (b) are critical.

    (c) take advantage of me.

    (d) are useful and fun to have around.

My parents...

    (a) are caring and supportive.

    (b) love me when I succeed.

    (c) give me what I need.

    (d) are the source of my genes.

I sometimes think that...

    (a) my source is infinite.

    (b) it is better to be spiritual than rich.

    (c) you need money to make it in life.

    (d) there is never enough ...

I have thought that:

    (a) My body is the outer expression of inner beauty.

    (b) On a scale of 1 to 10, I am a ...

    (c) People like me for my ...

    (d) When you look good, you feel good.

I often think:
   (a) I am free to love.
   (b) I thank God I'm not like ...
   (c) I can't help it; I just need to...
   (d) I'm only interested in results.

I could describe myself by saying:
   (a) I am loving.
   (b) I am a good judge.
   (c) I need people.
   (d) I have many things.

The (a) statements are affirmations of Life. They represent the seeds of thought you have sown.

                    Total # of seeds: _____

The (b) statements express a judgmental attitude which negates the seeds.

                    Total # of birds: _____

The (c) statements indicate a consciousness of dependency that over-shadows the seeds.

                    Total # of weeds: _____

The (d) statements are limited to facts and superficialities: a shallow mindedness.

                    Total # of stones: _____

   If each bird ate one seed, and each weed choked out one seed, and each rock hindered one seed from being well rooted, then how many seeds would be left to grow and bear fruit? Is it any wonder that our affirmations are ineffectual? Even so, it can bring forth 30, 60, 100 times more than you started with if even one seed remains.

BURIED TREASURE
Mt. 13:44

Again, the kingdom of heaven is like unto treasure hid in a
field; the which when a man hath found, he hideth, and for joy
thereof goeth and selleth all that he hath, and buyeth that field.

Kingdom of God

Most of the Jews who lived in the kingdom of Israel considered
it to be God's kingdom. However, Jesus did not. He usually made
it clear that when he spoke of God's kingdom, he was speaking of
the heavenly kingdom, not the geopolitical kingdom of Israel. He
located the kingdom of God within us. (See Lk. 17:20-21) He said
that his kingdom was not of this physical world. He described it as
a spiritual state of being. But because he used the Old Testament
prophecies of the kingdom of God to endorse his new teachings, it
was easy for those who were looking for an end to the Roman
occupation of Israel to confuse his revolutionary spiritual teachings
for an endorsement of revolution.

Jesus considered himself to be a spiritual being, not a physical
body. Therefore, I think it is likely that he and his disciples came to
consider the prophecies to be about a spiritual state, not a physical
place. Jesus did not view the prophecies of the kingdom as
analogies. He viewed his ministry as the actual fulfillment of those
prophecies, and he used parables (not prophecies) to provide
analogies of the kingdom. His use of analogy was necessary, for
the kingdom of heaven cannot be established by any means other
than spiritual realization.

Field

A field is a creative medium, where, normally, we sow seeds
and grow crops that prosper our life. Our field is where we work. It
is where we work with the Law, and It works for us according to

Its nature. It is where Life works within and through what we give It. The field is receptive, accepting, nurturing and creative. It is the source of increase and the setting for transformation. And when the field is likened to a spiritual state, the soil that makes up the field is analogous to what we call our soul, our mind, our consciousness; and the seeds sown in the soil are seeds of thought, belief, insight and inspiration. Jesus provided many parables of sowing and reaping, and working in the field, but this isn't one of them. This parable is not about the field. It is about the treasure that is within the field.

Treasure

A treasure has great value. There are many things in life that have great value, yet we do not treasure them all. That which we treasure has something more, something else, some other quality of value for us, something that distinguishes it from a mere valuable. Most valuables are only of value when sold, bartered, and exchanged. But treasure, or rather that which we treasure, has value in and of itself. It is something that gives value to our life by its mere presence in our life. Its value is so great that it is rendered priceless. It is not for sale. It is something we must keep. We cannot even give it away. Many treasured items have been given as gifts or inheritance, only to be discarded and ignored. Treasure must be found to be appreciated, or rather, that which is of value must be found, discovered, realized.
- A thing of beauty is not a treasure, but the beauty is.
- A symbol of freedom is not a national treasure, but freedom is.
- A keepsake is not a treasure, but the memory is.

The treasure, that is found and kept within, cannot be in the object of value. The treasure is the value we perceive within ourselves. Jesus said that once he found a treasure in the field, the man hid it, and then sold everything he had in order to buy the field. Why? Why hide the treasure? Why trade in everything you own in order to own the field? Well, perhaps the value of the field will appreciate over time, and everything else you own will depreciate. In fact, Jesus said as much.

- "Lay not up for yourselves treasures upon earth, where moth and rust doth corrupt, and where thieves break through and steal: But lay up for yourselves treasures in heaven, where neither moth nor rust doth corrupt, and where thieves do not break through nor steal: For where your treasure is, there will your heart be also." (Mt. 6:19-21)

But aside from the wise investment aspect of it, we have to own the field because that is where the treasure is. The treasure is hidden in the field and cannot be taken from the field. To own the treasure, one must own the field. It is part and parcel of it. Remember, the field is intangible. The field is within, as well as around us. It is the consciousness in which we live, move, and work with Life. The field represents one's consciousness of Life, and once we find a treasure within, Jesus likens that to heaven. To be in and of the kingdom of heaven is to be conscious of the inner treasure. It is an awareness that has greater value than all the things we value in life.

To be kept within the field of consciousness, the treasure must be intangible. It must be the essence, or the presence, of that which makes life valuable. What might that treasure be? I've already suggested that it could be beauty or freedom. I could suggest that the treasure is Love, or Peace of Mind, or Illumination, awareness of our oneness with God. These are all holy treasures which if kept within make life worth living. But I cannot say what anyone should search for, or what they might find. A treasure has value for the one who finds it, by virtue of finding it within themselves. It is in this sense that the intangible treasure of Life will always be buried treasure, for we must find it within, and keep it to ourselves.

ONE PEARL
Mt. 13:45-46

Again, the kingdom of heaven is like unto a merchant man, seeking goodly pearls; Who, when he had found one pearl of great price, went and sold all that he had, and bought it.

Great Price
This parable is similar to the parable of the buried treasure, in that both equate attaining a heavenly consciousness with acquiring something of great value. In both parables we are told that we must let go of that which has less value, or little to no value, in order to hold onto that which has greater value. And, both parables address the price we must pay to attain that greater good: it will take everything you've got.

In each case, a man sold all that he owned in order to purchase what he perceived to be of greater value. Their's was not an act of sacrifice; it was an investment. He didn't lose anything in the exchange; he gained everything. In one parable, a buried treasure was acquired, and in the other parable, a pearl. Each profited beyond what it cost them to make such a wise purchase. That is why they did it: for the profit, the enrichment, the greater value.

Poverty
This parable does not recommend that we sell all that we have in order to live in poverty. A transaction that results in acquiring a buried treasure or a pearl of great price can hardly be thought of as resulting in poverty. The transaction did require that they put in all that they had, but that resulted in a profit. They gained more than they had to start with, more than they would have had if they had not gone all in. The same lesson is taught in the parables of sowing and reaping: you sow all that you have, and then you reap more than you sowed. Do not make the mistake of jumping in and out of

the context of the parable when trying to learn its lesson. Do not think that this parable equates financial investment with spiritual gain. If it did, that would be fraud.

We are right to be offended by the suggestion that we should, or could, impoverish ourselves to gain spiritual value, but the parable doesn't suggest that. The merchant didn't spend all his money to gain the kingdom of heaven. He didn't trade all his tangible assets in on an intangible value. He was a pearl merchant, and he bought a pearl. He liquidated all of his assets so that he could buy more, and the suggestion is that he made a wise and profitable purchase.

Profit

Jesus once asked: "For what shall it profit a man, if he shall gain the whole world, and lose his own soul?" (Mk. 8:36) I think we know the answer: there is no profit in that. We know that financial wealth is no substitute for spiritual enrichment. We know that we cannot buy knowledge, love, security, freedom, happiness and well-being. We know this; don't we?

Apparently not; for most people work long and hard in order to feel secure, to think of themselves as successful, to be loved and appreciated by others. Marketing experts agree that most people are motivated by the lure of intangibles. We think that if we gain the world that we'll profit our soul; but it doesn't work out that way. Being profitable does not have the same value as spiritual enrichment. But that doesn't mean that being profitable results in the loss of one's soul either.

There is no profit in losing your soul (your mind, yourself, your self-worth), but neither is there any spiritual gain in forsaking a profitable life. Regardless of what frustrated people in dead-end jobs think, you can't sell your soul for money! You can ignore it, but that is not what you are being paid to do. Regardless of what anyone with their hand out says, you cannot profit your soul by giving away, losing, or using your money. Your soul must be full before the act of giving can be fulfilling. We can enrich our soul, and we can be profitable. You may value one currency more than the other, but you'll have to use both just to get by in the world. But while trying to do just that, we often make the mistake of equating prosperity with enrichment, money with security, success with achievement. They are not the same, and one is not the cause of the other! Spiritual wealth has great value, but it is not prosperity; and while the simple life is well worth living, a life of poverty costs far too much. If I could buy my way into heaven, I would. What a bargain that would be; but it is impossible to enter in by any means other than becoming conscious of it. "… behold, the kingdom of God is within you." (Lk. 17:21)

Trust

The real issue is not how many things we have, but where we place our trust. We affirm that it is In God We Trust, even as we spend our cash. Jesus pointed out that we should layup treasure in heaven. (See Mt. 6:19-21) He also taught that we should trust in the Lord and invest our inner talents.

When instead, we rely on our possessions, we tend to get possessive and become possessed and obsessed with things. Things get in the way of acquiring our buried treasure and maintaining our true wealth. However, it is not things, but our trust in them, that is the problem.

This parable brings to mind the story of the rich young fool (See Mt. 19:16-23). He asked Jesus what good deeds he might do to acquire eternal life. He wasn't asking to be immortal, or how to live a spiritually fulfilling life. He was wondering how to get into heaven. He told Jesus he was abiding by all of the laws and commandments of Moses, and doing all that Jesus had suggested. He asked what more he could do, as if that wasn't enough. He was already doing more than enough, yet he still felt incomplete and unfulfilled. In filling his day, he was overlooking the fullness of his

Life. It is rather like not seeing the forest for all the trees, when you have to ask for directions to the kingdom of heaven that is within you. I would have told him that there was nothing more that he could do, for he was doing too much already. It is sometimes necessary to do less so that one can be more. Do less, to be more aware. I would have advised him to stop, to look within, and listen. Jesus advised him to divest himself of all he had invested himself in so that he might realize the treasure to be found within. "If thou wilt be perfect, go *and* sell that thou hast, and give to the poor, and thou shalt have treasure in heaven: and come and follow me." We are told that the young man went away sorrowfully: "for he had great possessions."

What could he do? His possessions possessed him. His holdings had a hold on him. Jesus' advice did not make sense because the rich young fool was asking about a future event, while Jesus was speaking of a present reality. It's not money, but the love of money, that gets in our way. It is not possessions, but being possessive that gets in the way. Some suggest that if you do without things, you will learn to do without, and you won't miss a thing. They must also think that ignorance is bliss. Poverty doesn't enrich one's life. There are plenty of people who are doing without money and things that are considered the bare minimum for survival, and they are no better off for it. It's not what you are doing without, but what you find within that enriches your life. To put things right in our life, we need to put first things first.

- First, find it. Find the pearl of great price, the buried treasure; and then, divest yourself of all that gets in the way of acquiring it.
- First there must be a shift in consciousness, and then there will be a corresponding change in the conditions of your life.
- First, change your mind; then change your behavior.

Faith

It is only when we have found that which is of great value, that it will be possible to divest ourselves of that which is of a lesser value; not things necessarily, but thoughts, beliefs and opinions that have little value. The judgments and facts we put such great stock in must be liquidated. That is the price we must pay to realize a greater good. For example, you may know what you would do, and know what others should do, but if you would know respect, then do not tell them what to do. You can have love for another, but you cannot entrust your love to them. You cannot expect them to think and act as you would. Love is something each must find within and keep in confidence. You can do unto others as you would have them do unto you, but you do not expect them to do unto you as you would do unto them. You may belong to a particular faith, believing and accepting a great many things as a condition of membership in that faith. You may have great faith in God, or Jesus, or some other holy being, but that is a poor substitute for the greater faith: simply being faithful.

There are no faith-healers. It wasn't Jesus' faith that healed the sick. Jesus never said that his faith healed anyone. He often said that their own faith had made them whole. Faith is always found within, or it isn't faith. Do not confuse reliance on others for faith. It is done unto us according to our faith, be it little or great. When speaking of the Roman Centurion, Jesus said: "I have not found so great faith, no, not in Israel." (Mt. 8:10, Lk. 7:9) That must have offended members of Jesus' faith. Jesus was impressed with the soldiers faith; not because he had come to Jesus requesting prayer (which would have indicated a faith in Jesus), but because, as one commander in a chain of command, the Centurion had an understanding of a higher authority. The Centurion had faith in the command of one who spoke his word with that authority. He knew Jesus to be a man of faith because he was himself a man of faith.

Jesus praised those who had faith and attributed their results to their own faith. He was also critical of those, who having no faith of their own, wished to rely on his faith. He was especially critical of his disciples for exhibiting little or no faith of their own. They could not have a greater faith as long as they held onto their faith in Jesus. To have the greater good, and do the greater deeds, they must have the faith of Jesus, rather than faith in Jesus.

- The price of self-reliance is that we give up our dependence on others.
- The price of freedom is that we give up control.
- The price of faith is that we no longer entertain our fears.

These qualities of thought and consciousness are indeed pearls of great price, and well worth it.

THE FOOLISH and THE WISE
Mt. 25:1-13

Then shall the kingdom of heaven be likened unto ten virgins which took their lamps, and went forth to meet the bridegroom. And five of them were wise, and five were foolish. They that were foolish took their lamps, and took no oil with them: But the wise took oil in their vessels with their lamps. While the bridegroom tarried, they all slumbered and slept. And at midnight there was a cry made, "Behold, the bridegroom cometh; go ye out to meet him." Then all those virgins arose, and trimmed their lamps. And the foolish said unto the wise, "Give us of your oil; for our lamps are gone out." But the wise answered, saying, "Not so; lest there be not enough for us and you: but go ye rather to them that sell, and buy for yourselves." And while they went to buy, the bridegroom came; and they that were ready went in with him to the marriage: and the door was shut. Afterward came also the other virgins, saying, "Lord, Lord, open to us." But he answered and said, "Verily I say unto you, I know you not." Watch therefore, for ye know neither the day nor the hour wherein the Son of man cometh.

Moral of the Story

We may again look to the last verse for the moral of this story: Life is full of surprises; which can be unpleasant for those who are ill prepared for them. At all times be prepared to fulfill your role in life, for you never know when you will be called on.

Preparedness, vigilance, faithfulness, etc., is a recurring message in the teachings of Jesus; as is its counterpoint: disappointment. Many are called, but few are chosen. Few are chosen if the many are not prepared to enter into the joy of Life. Many think they are ready and willing, and are understandably disappointed when they think that they are not among the chosen few. However, the reality is that they did not choose to enter in. It is not that they would not choose to enter in but that they did not make the choices that result in being ready. It is foolish to think that you were not chosen, and wise to realize that you have made other choices. Our experience in life, and of Life, is equal to the choices we make for and about our self. We must be equal to an opportunity for it to be ours.

Hidden Meaning

Well, equal opportunity is what the story means to me. My insight is not the moral of the story, but a hidden meaning, revealed by the telling of the story, awaiting recognition by one who already knows what it means. The meaning of the parable is not hidden in the parable. The meaning is within me. It may be recognized in the parable, but it is realized within me. It is what I learn from the parable because it is what I already know, or think I know. If I think that there is an affinity between Jesus and me, an agreement between what he taught and what I believe, then I might be foolish enough to think the parable was written with my meaning in mind. But I'm not that foolish. The parable reminds me of what I believe. My beliefs need only be true to me, and I to them.

The Point

If the moral is stated in the last verse, and the meaning is already known within you, what is the point of the story? Some think that parables are just a memorable and colorful way of making a simple point. But, it is only a simple point if you already know it. Is a parable to serve only as a reminder? Is there nothing else we can get from this parable? I think there is more to it than that.

Though the parable reminds me of other verses from the teachings of Jesus, they also introduce concepts I did not know or think of before. The parables are lessons to learn. All teaching is building upon fundamentals that we already know, and this is what a parable does best. The characters and plot provide the building blocks for a new mental construct. I am of the opinion that parables are about learning experiences, and if you learn the lessons they teach you can avoid some of the experiences that life has in store for those who are not so well versed.

Ten Virgins

So, what else can we learn from this parable? What are we to make of ten virgins waiting up late for a bridegroom? Some Biblical scholars translate virgin as maiden, stating that the term refers to youth and inexperience. Following this line of thinking, some consider the ten virgins to be bridesmaids, not brides. Some manuscripts state that they came with their lamps to meet the bridegroom and the bride. Regardless of the implications and connotations of "virgin," the fact that there were ten of them makes that designation inconsequential. It is not important to the parable whether virginity refers to piety or propriety. It simply says that they were all equally acceptable, equal to the opportunity: the call to celebrate a marriage. The only distinction amongst the ten is that five were wise, and five were foolish.

The ten were to function as a welcoming committee. They had oil burning lamps to light the way to the wedding, but the groom delayed, and as they waited, they fell asleep. While they slept, their lamps burned out. Their function as light bearers and way-showers would be impossible if they didn't replenish their shallow lamps with oil from deeper vessels. Without their lights, they would walk in darkness, and as such they would not be able to fulfill their role. They would not be ready to enter into the wedding celebration.

- The five foolish ones would gladly have lit the way, if there had been no delay, but they were not prepared to provide light throughout the night. They were as shallow as their lamps.
- The five wise ones had prepared themselves by bringing extra oil. They had a depth of understanding to draw upon that the fools did not have. They had prepared for a delay. They were prepared to sustain themselves from their own reserves.

A Confidence

This parable points out the importance of developing one's inner resources, inner knowledge, insight that proves to be wisdom. Such knowledge is always held in confidence. It is a personal consciousness of faith, not the shared faith of religion or tradition. It is not faith in others, or in what others say. It is not an awareness that one can share with another. It has a hidden meaning. We cannot tell others what we know of the inner presence, our spiritual essence, and if we attempt to explain it, they gain no understanding. The wise did not share their oil because they could not, and if they had tried, it would not have done the foolish any good.

A Clue

The wise seem rather harsh when telling the foolish to get a clue, buy a vowel, go to the market and purchase some understanding. There are plenty of people trying to sell what they know to those who know no better. Life is harsh when you search in vain, asking others for what they cannot give. That which has already been given to you can only be found within you. The foolish might be able to purchase enough to top off their oil lamps, and have light for a while again, but the similarity between the foolish and the wise is superficial. The foolish lack a depth of knowledge that provides the inner resourcefulness to understand their situation and choose wisely. It is because they lack an inner knowledge that they cannot enter into the celebration of Life, the marriage feast. It is not because of the delay that their lights burned out, but because they were not prepared to rely on their inner resources. The wise did not keep them out, but neither could they provide them with what it takes to enter in. It was not the bridegroom who shut them out, but the fact that they were not known, not proven, not ready and able to enter in. The door was shut to the foolish because a personal preparedness, of a sort that results in confidence and self-reliance, is required to enter into the consciousness of Oneness.

Consciousness of Life

But, let's not forget that the parable is about the kingdom of heaven, a spiritual state of being. The parables can provide insights and clues for living a more fulfilling life, but they are not a guide to daily living. They are not the stories of many people, but of one person. They do not describe a future reality, but the present reality of our life. They describe a state of consciousness, that encompasses all that we think and believe, see and perceive, the actual as well as the potential. All of the parables of the kingdom describe joy and sorrow, wheat and weeds, wisdom and foolishness, the Father's house and the far country.

In this parable, the kingdom of heaven is not compared to a marriage, but to the whole situation leading up to and including it. The parable states that: "Then shall the kingdom of heaven be likened unto ten virgins which took their lamps, and went forth to meet the bridegroom." The kingdom includes all ten virgins, not just the five who got in the door. The kingdom of heaven is not a gated community. It is not a separate reality for those who happen upon it, or are wise enough to wait for it. Don't confuse fulfillment in life for merely living, or for Life Itself. Even those who live unfulfilled lives exist within the one Life, the infinite reality, in which we live, move and have our being.

Celebration of Life

In the parables, marriage symbolizes a spiritual union, a realization whereby two become as one. The conscious awareness becomes one with consciousness, establishing a greater self-awareness. The spirit becomes one with the soul, establishing a sense of wholeness and well-being. The bridegroom becomes one with the bride, and where there was a sense of two separate beings, there is now the recognition of one. But who is the bride? That is the one character never spoken of, yet central to the story. If you can deduce who the bride is, then you'll be able to understand what the other characters in the parable represent; and only then will you be able to grasp the meaning of this parable.

I know that most Biblical scholars focus on the bridegroom, and define the other roles accordingly. They think the bridegroom represents Jesus (or the Christ), and they read the parable as a puzzle that we are to solve to discover our relationship with Jesus. But Jesus said that this was a parable about the kingdom of heaven. Are we to believe that getting into the kingdom of heaven is just a matter of having a good relationship with Jesus? And if so;
- Are we to aspire to being a bride?
- Are the foolish those who don't know and don't accept that Jesus is the bridegroom?
- Are the wise those who are ready and wait for Jesus' return?

Most scholars think that the foolish virgins represent those of us who let our light go out because we have doubts rather than a deep reservoir of faith, such as the wise virgins possess. Some even think this parable predicts that half of us will get into heaven, and half will be shut out. *(Those are the best odds I ever heard!)*

But still, the question remains: Who is the bride? It can't be one of the five wise virgins, or all of them. The Jews were not practicing or endorsing polygamy, yet the only ones to get past the door were the bridegroom and the wise virgins. The reasonable

164

conclusion is that the bride was already there, always there, waiting here, inside.

In this parable of the kingdom, the marriage celebration is an acknowledgment of the union of the individual spirit with the universal soul. It is a celebration of love and light for we can see that we are one. In this parable, marriage represents the consciousness of oneness with the infinite One, the merging of the individual with the Universal. It is this consciousness that allows us to proclaim as Jesus did: "I and *my* Father are one." (Jn. 10:30)

- "The first of all the commandments is, Hear, O Israel; The Lord our God is one Lord: And thou shalt love the Lord thy God with all thy heart, and with all thy soul, and with all thy mind, and with all thy strength: this is the first commandment." (Mk. 12:29-30, Deu. 6:4)

Light of Wisdom

This parable describes the situation where wisdom would lead you through the door while foolishness would leave you knocking at the door. The door opens and closes upon the marriage celebration, a celebration of Love. The door is an opportunity, and it requires wisdom to light your way to it. Within the kingdom is wisdom and foolishness, light and darkness, the opportunity to enter into the celebration, or to be disappointed. Where there is an opportunity, there is a choice, and where there is a choice, there is freedom and the consequences that go with it.

I think this is a parable about fulfillment. The light of wisdom burns night and day if our lamp is constantly full; and our life is a celebration if we continuously fulfill it. I don't think this parable can be reduced to a missive from Jesus: Keep the light burning for my return. I don't think the parable is a prediction of a second coming. I find it to be instruction in what it takes to behold the inner kingdom. It takes the light of wisdom.

ABOUT THE AUTHOR

Kyle Canyon / Mt. Charleston, NV 1968

Glenn Edward Chaffin (pictured here leading a youth retreat) has studied and taught New Thought principles for well over forty-five years. He has been an avid student and proponent of the writings and philosophy of Ralph Waldo Emerson and Ernest Holmes since 1967. Their teachings provide the foundation for his understanding of the teachings of Jesus. In 1975, Rev. Chaffin began his ministry in Minnesota, where he resides with his wife, three children and three grandchildren.

Made in the USA
Middletown, DE
04 June 2018